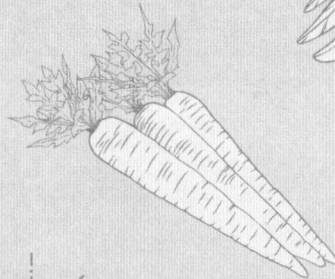

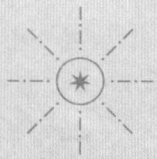

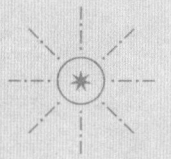

FROM THE FILMS OF

Harry Potter | FANTASTIC BEASTS

— OFFICIAL —

WIZARDING WORLD

COOKBOOK

PLEASE
KEEP OFF THE
DIRIGIBLE
PLUMS

FROM THE FILMS OF

Harry Potter | FANTASTIC BEASTS

OFFICIAL

WIZARDING WORLD

COOKBOOK

SPELLBINDING MEALS FROM NEW YORK TO HOGWARTS AND BEYOND!

Recipes by Sarah Walker-Caron & Elena P. Craig
Written by Jody Revenson

WIZARDING WORLD

greenfinch

Created by Insight Editions, LP

INSIGHT EDITIONS

SAN RAFAEL · LOS ANGELES · LONDON

CONTENTS

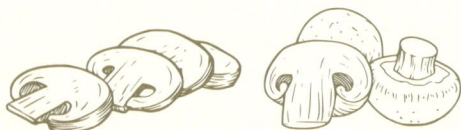

Chapter Three
GREAT HALL FEASTS

Chapter Four
NEW YORK CITY

Chapter Five
PARIS

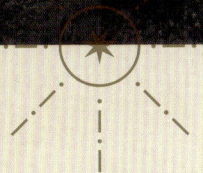

INTRODUCTION

The culinary aspect of the wizarding world has greatly expanded since its first appearance on-screen in *Harry Potter and the Philosopher's Stone*, where we met Harry Potter serving up breakfast from Aunt Petunia and Uncle Vernon's kitchen at Number Four, Privet Drive, in Little Whinging, England. Fortunately, Harry received his acceptance letter to Hogwarts School of Witchcraft and Wizardry soon afterwards, and his own world grew exponentially. He was taken by the Hogwarts Keeper of Keys and Grounds, Rubeus Hagrid, to the hidden wizarding marketplace Diagon Alley in London, which serves its magical populace sumptuous soups and other pub fare at The Leaky Cauldron. Harry's journey with his best friends, Ron Weasley and Hermione Granger, took them from parties and feasts at their school in Scotland, to cosy breakfasts in the Weasley family's home, The Burrow, to meetings of the Order of the Phoenix held in the kitchen of Harry's godfather Sirius Black's house, Grimmauld Place and even to the streets of Muggle-filled London, with its coffee shops and cafés.

In an earlier time, Magizoologist Newt Scamander travelled to New York City after researching his book *Fantastic Beasts and Where to Find Them*. There he met the talented 'kitchen witches' Tina and Queenie Goldstein and the No-Maj baker Jacob Kowalski. Their adventures took them from New York to England and then to Paris, Germany and beyond.

Harry Potter: Official Wizarding World Cookbook offers cuisine from many of these places, for magical dishes ranging from Diagon Alley Steak and Ale Pie to the Goldstein Sisters' Hot Chocolate Mug Cakes. Other offerings include Great Hall Sweet French Toast with Berry Compote, Luchino Caffe Picante Paninis, and a Hogsmeade-inspired Ginger and Lime Butterscotch Mug drink.

The Great Hall of Hogwarts is known for its sumptuous feasts, whether they're for the Start-of-Term gathering, with the inspired Drumsticks with Fluffy Feast Rolls and Corn with Garlic and Parmesan, or the End-of-Year farewell, honoured here with the End-of-Year Feast Beef Short Ribs with Yorkshire Pudding and Buttery Diced Carrots.

The meals served in the Great Hall are the best of comfort foods, with roasted meats and an endless number of mouthwatering side dishes such as Floating Candles Herb Butter–Brushed Corn the Cob and Sorting Hat Ceremony Peas, Bacon and Diced Onions.

Celebrations and parties are also included. Join the Slug Club and enjoy Professor Slughorn's Dinner Party Sausage Rolls or Slug Club Prawn and Chorizo Skewers. Also on offer are Halloween Pumpkin Carrot Squares and Hogwarts Hot Mulled Pumpkin Cider for chilly autumn evenings. In the spirit of the Triwizard Tournament, try the Yule Ball Sherbet Fizzy. And remember, chocolate in the wizarding world isn't just for a snack or dessert – it's actually helpful after an encounter with Dementors, so the Triwizard Tournament Chocolate Roulade and the All Better Now Chocolate Cakes are here to boost both spirits and sweet tooths.

Newt Scamander and Jacob Kowalski travel to 1930s Paris to locate both Credence Barebone and Tina Goldstein in *Fantastic Beasts: The Crimes of Grindelwald*. The pavements of the Place Cachée, a wizarding marketplace akin to Britain's Diagon Alley, are lined with patisseries and cafés. Ideas for Parisian-style cuisine include a Zouwu Cheese Soufflé and Teddy the Niffler's Pouch Stuffed Tomatoes. Nicolas Flamel's Caramelized Onion Galette has a sweet and savoury taste that's one for the ages.

And to epitomize Newt's adventures in New York City, there's the Niffler Babies' Everything Chicken Wings and Tina Goldstein's Ultimate New York Hot Dog. For a refresher, try The Blind Pig Laughing Lemonade Cocktails, and give it a sweet accompaniment with Kowalski Bakery's Fluffy Cinnamon Buns with Vanilla Bean Glaze.

Each easy-to-follow recipe includes vegan, vegetarian and gluten-free notations, with consideration towards everybody's dietary needs. Plus, you will find suggestions for easy ingredient substitutions, along with cooking and baking tricks.

The recipes within this book offer an enticing panoply of cuisine that will enchant family, friends, partygoers and guests with magical meals from all parts of the wizarding world.

Chapter One

LONDON, LITTLE WHINGING & THE BURROW

DUDLEY DURSLEY'S SWIRLY TAIL BACON CHEDDAR BREADSTICKS

★
YIELD: 6 breadsticks | PREP TIME: 15 minutes | COOK TIME: 30 minutes

To avoid receiving anymore of Hogwarts acceptance letters for his nephew, Harry Potter, Vernon Dursley hides away his family at the Hut-on-the-Rock in *Harry Potter and the Philosopher's Stone*. As Vernon, Petunia and their son, Dudley, sleep, Harry draws a cake with candles on the dirt floor. At midnight, he makes a wish, for it is his birthday. Suddenly, the hut's door bangs open and half-giant Rubeus Hagrid appears. He hands Harry a birthday cake and his acceptance letter to Hogwarts.

While Harry talks with Hagrid and learns he's a wizard, Dudley grabs the boxed cake and begins to feast. Hagrid notices this and punishes him by giving him a swirly pig's tail.

These puff pastry breadsticks, with their own swirl as a nod to this iconic scene, have a hint of caramelization that comes from the brown sugar cooking next to the bacon. Savoury Cheddar rounds out the flavour.

Flour, for dusting

1 sheet frozen puff pastry, thawed

1 tablespoon soft light brown sugar

6 rashers bacon

30g Cheddar cheese, grated

Preheat the oven to 200°C/180°C fan/Gas Mark 6. Line a baking sheet with baking paper and set aside.

Dust a large chopping board with flour and lay out the puff pastry. Spread the brown sugar evenly over it. Lay the bacon rashers on top so they are touching but not overlapping. Use a sharp knife to cut the puff pastry into 6 strips, using the bacon as a guide. Scatter the Cheddar cheese evenly over the strips.

Working with one strip at a time, twist the puff pastry around the bacon. Continue twisting on the diagonal, encapsulating the filling with the dough until the whole strip has been folded. Transfer the strip to the prepared baking sheet. Continue until all the dough has been used.

Place the baking sheet in the oven and bake for 20–25 minutes or until the pastry is golden brown and puffed. Remove from the oven. The breadsticks should be eaten hot.

These are delightful served with Leaky Cauldron Tomato Chicken Stew (see page 19).

★ **BEHIND THE MAGIC** ★

The graphic and prop departments peppered the shelves of the Dursley home with Dudley's certificates of achievement. One of these – the Headteacher's Award – was for 'always eating up his lunch'.

'OH, UM, I'D APPRECIATE IT IF YOU DIDN'T TELL ANYONE AT HOGWARTS ABOUT THAT. STRICTLY SPEAKING, I'M NOT ALLOWED TO DO MAGIC.'

– Rubeus Hagrid, *Harry Potter and the Philosopher's Stone*

XENOPHILIUS LOVEGOOD'S TEA BREAD

✳

V | YIELD: 1 loaf | PREP TIME: 15 minutes | COOK TIME: 1 hour 5 minutes

---

In *Harry Potter and the Deathly Hallows – Part 1*, Harry sees Xenophilius Lovegood, editor of *The Quibbler*, wearing a pendant with the symbol of the Deathly Hallows. Harry, Ron and Hermione visit his home as they pursue information about these three powerful magical objects to defeat Voldemort, unaware that his daughter, Luna, has been kidnapped by the Death Eaters.

To get Luna back, Xenophilius must turn Harry over to the Death Eaters. 'He's put in a terrible position where he's championed Harry Potter's cause all Harry's life,' says Rhys Ifans (Xenophilius), 'and he's faced with this gargantuan dilemma. He's jumpy and busy and eccentric, but not mad.'

Dotted with dried dried currants and almonds and infused with the fragrance of English breakfast tea, this herby loaf is perfect for teatime, breakfast or brunch. Perhaps if Xenophilius had been a little less stressed when Luna's friends visited him, he would have served this.

Ingredients

- Butter or oil, for greasing
- 2 teabags English breakfast tea
- 300ml boiling water
- 2 medium eggs
- 75g soft light brown sugar
- Zest of 1 lemon (about 1 tablespoon)
- 1 teaspoon vanilla extract
- 315g plain flour
- 1 tablespoon baking powder
- ½ teaspoon coarse salt
- 75g dried currants
- 50g flaked almonds

Method

Preheat the oven to 180°C/160°C fan/Gas Mark 4. Thoroughly grease a loaf tin.

Add the teabags to boiling water in a mug or a glass jug and infuse for 10 minutes. You want the tea to be very strong.

Meanwhile, whisk together the eggs in a large mixing bowl until smooth. Add the brown sugar, lemon zest and vanilla extract and whisk well to combine.

Remove the teabags from the tea. Very slowly, add the tea to the egg mixture, whisking constantly as you go.

Add the flour, baking powder and salt to the bowl. Fold in until just combined. Then add the dried currants and almonds, stirring until just combined. Pour the mixture into the prepared loaf tin and tap gently to smooth out.

Place the loaf tin into the oven and bake for 55–65 minutes or until a knife inserted in the centre comes out clean.

✳ BEHIND THE MAGIC ✳

The graphics department created seven issues of *The Quibbler,* and more than seven hundred copies of each issue were printed. Many of these lay heaped on the floor of the Lovegood house.

'AH, BUT YOUR TEA'S GROWN COLD…'

– Xenophilius Lovegood,
Harry Potter and the Deathly Hallows – Part 1

ON THE RUN FLAPJACKS

✦

V, GF | YIELD: 8 servings | PREP TIME: 10 minutes | COOK TIME: 40 minutes

---

When Voldemort and the Death Eaters take over the Ministry of Magic in *Harry Potter and the Deathly Hallows – Part 1*, Harry, Ron and Hermione go on the run. Eventually, they encounter Snatchers, mercenaries sent to find them. The trio races through the forest to escape, leading to some competitive stunt work by the actors. Director David Yates had to take them aside and remind them that the scene was not about who could run the fastest. 'I didn't realize I was going that fast,' says Rupert Grint (Ron), 'but they actually told me to slow down because I was beating Emma.' 'Rupert can move very quickly,' concedes Daniel Radcliffe (Harry), 'but Emma and I are both quite fast across the ground.'

These flapjacks include chocolate chips and dried cranberries, making them a delicious snack that Hermione might pack for the trio's journey. The chocolate chips melt into these bars, infusing them with chocolaty flavour. Store them in a reusable container for the best results at home or when transporting.

225g unsalted butter, cut into pieces

225g soft light brown sugar

1 tablespoon golden syrup

300g porridge oats

85g mini chocolate chips

75g dried cranberries

Preheat the oven to 160°C/140°C fan/Gas Mark 3. Line a 30 x 23cm baking sheet with baking paper.

In a large saucepan set over a low heat, heat the butter together with the brown sugar and golden syrup, stirring constantly.

Remove from heat and stir in the oats, mini chocolate chips and cranberries until combined. The chocolate will melt.

Spread the mixture on to the prepared baking sheet using a rubber spatula, taking care to press it into one even layer.

Place the baking sheet in the oven and bake for 30 minutes. Then remove from the oven and leave to cool for 10 minutes before transferring the paper and flapjacks to a chopping board. Cut into 7.5 x 2.5cm pieces.

Cool completely. For best results, the flapjacks should be stored in an airtight container, with greaseproof paper separating the layers.

✦ **BEHIND THE MAGIC** ✦

After the chase scene in *Harry Potter and the Deathly Hallows – Part 1* Emma Watson (Hermione) said she 'definitely gave the boys a good run for their money.'

'WELL, DON'T HANG ABOUT. SNATCH 'EM!'

– Scabior, *Harry Potter and the Deathly Hallows – Part 1*

LEAKY CAULDRON TOMATO CHICKEN STEW

YIELD: 4–6 servings | PREP TIME: 15 minutes | COOK TIME: 8¼ hours

---

In *Harry Potter and the Philosopher's Stone*, Rubeus Hagrid, Keeper of Keys and Grounds at Hogwarts, brings his charge, Harry Potter, to The Leaky Cauldron for a warming dinner after their day in Diagon Alley picking up school supplies. There he fills Harry in on the heroism of his parents against Voldemort and tells him why he is so important to the wizarding world.

Inside The Leaky Cauldron is a large dining area and a huge blazing fireplace (home of the cauldron that leaks). The walls are made of plastered-over brick, long wood beams line the ceiling and the windows have a trefoil design, all marks of the Tudor style of the 1500s.

This take on a dish that might be served at this wizarding tavern and inn is a hearty tomato-based stew with chunks of potatoes, kale, carrots and chicken – perfect after a long day shopping in Diagon Alley.

- 675g boneless, skinless chicken breasts, cut into 2.5cm cubes
- 2 tablespoons flour
- 1 medium brown onion, diced
- 450g Maris Piper potatoes, cut into 1cm cubes
- 450g carrots, diced
- 3 cloves garlic, very finely chopped
- 400g passata
- 1½ teaspoons salt
- 1 teaspoon pepper
- 1 bay leaf
- 1 teaspoon dried thyme
- 1 teaspoon dried rosemary
- 750ml chicken stock
- 150g frozen peas
- 75g fresh kale, chopped

In a large bowl, combine the chicken cubes and the flour, tossing well. Transfer to the bowl of a slow cooker. Add the onions, potatoes, carrots, garlic, passata, salt, pepper, bay leaf, thyme, rosemary and chicken stock. Stir.

Set the slow cooker to low and cook for 8 hours.

Add the peas and kale to the slow cooker and cook for a further 10–15 minutes or until warmed. Serve. This is delightful with the Shell Cottage Seed Bread (see page 47).

HOB METHOD:
To cook this on the hob, you need a 5-litre or larger casserole; also add 1 tablespoon rapeseed oil to the recipe. Begin by heating the oil in the casserole on the hob over a medium heat. In a large mixing bowl, toss the chicken with the flour and add to the pot. Cook, stirring once, for 4–5 minutes or until opaque. Add the onions, potatoes, carrots, garlic, passata, salt, pepper, bay leaf, thyme, rosemary and chicken stock to the pot. Stir well. Reduce the heat to medium-low, cover and cook for 45 minutes, stirring once or twice. Add the peas and kale to the pot and cook for a further 10 minutes. Taste and adjust the seasonings as desired. Serve immediately.

> 'FIRST. AND UNDERSTAND THIS. HARRY.
> 'CAUSE IT'S VERY IMPORTANT. NOT ALL WIZARDS
> ARE GOOD. SOME OF THEM GO BAD.'
>
> – Rubeus Hagrid, *Harry Potter and the Philosopher's Stone*

HARRY POTTER'S LATE NIGHT SPLIT PEA SOUP

V, V+*, GF | YIELD: 8 servings | PREP TIME: 20 minutes

Harry leaves Privet Drive after inflating his uncle's sister, Harry's Aunt Marge, in *Harry Potter and the Prisoner of Azkaban*. He takes the Knight Bus to The Leaky Cauldron and is greeted by Cornelius Fudge, the Minister of Magic, who offers him a bowl of pea soup.

Production designer Stuart Craig deliberately chose to decorate the interior of The Leaky Cauldron in the Tudor style of the 1500s, to reinforce his philosophy that 'the wizarding world has a different timescale'.

Harry was actually warned off having the pea soup after he was rescued by the Knight Bus. If the pea soup served to Harry had been this one, he more than likely would have accepted. Split peas create a lovely texture and add just the right flavour for this recipe, featuring cashew nuts for added protein and an exceptional creaminess.

- 1 litre vegetable stock
- 125g roasted, salted cashew nuts
- 2 tablespoons olive oil
- 30g unsalted butter
- 2 leeks, rinsed, quartered, and thinly sliced
- 2 celery sticks, finely chopped
- 4 cloves garlic, very finely chopped
- 1 teaspoon coarse salt, or more as needed (see note)
- 900g frozen peas
- 250ml double cream
- Pepper
- 75g hulled pumpkin seeds, for garnish (optional)
- ¼ teaspoon chilli flakes, for garnish (optional)

SPECIALIST TOOLS
- Casserole or large saucepan
- Stick blender or stand blender

In a large microwave-safe jug or bowl, add 500ml of the vegetable stock and the cashew nuts. Microwave for 2 minutes and set aside to soak until needed.

In a large casserole over a medium-high heat, add the olive oil and butter. When the butter begins to foam, add the leeks, celery, garlic and salt. Sauté until the vegetables are tender, about 10 minutes.

Add the remaining 500ml of stock, the cashew nut mixture and the peas. Bring to the boil over a medium-high heat and boil until the peas start to break apart, about 15 minutes. Stir in the double cream, and use the stick blender to blend until smooth. Taste; add more salt if needed and pepper as desired. Cook a further 5 minutes or until heated through. Serve in bowls with a scattering of pumpkin seeds and chilli flakes, if using. This dish pairs well with Shell Cottage Seed Bread (see page 47) or Nimbus 2000 Toasted Parmesan Brooms with Pine Nut Roasted Garlic Hummus (see page 66).

> ✷ **NOTES**
>
> If you don't have a stick blender, remove the soup from the heat, allow to cool for 10 minutes and carefully transfer the soup, in small batches, to a stand blender; purée until smooth. Return to the pot, season and reheat.
>
> This can easily be made vegan by using coconut butter (or another butter substitute) and a dairy-free option such as oat or almond milk in the place of double cream.
>
> Missing the beasts in this meal? Adding 225–350g of diced ham would be a traditional choice. Dice the meat and add it after blending the soup. Bring the soup back to a simmer and cook for about 10 minutes or until heated through.

HERMIONE GRANGER'S EXTENSION CHARM BACON AND POTATO PASTIES

✴

YIELD: 8 pasties | PREP TIME: 15 minutes | COOK TIME: 45 minutes

Spurred on by the threat of Voldemort and his Death Eaters in *Harry Potter and the Deathly Hallows – Part 1*, Hermione packs a change of clothes and other essentials in a magical bag, in case she, Ron and Harry need to go on the run.

Graphic designers Miraphora Mina and Eduardo Lima put together a list of the books they thought Hermione would find helpful during their travels. 'It was a really nice opportunity to think, well, which ones would she have taken on her trip?' says Mina. 'There was a line in the script that described her bag. She shakes it, and there is this terrible noise of stacked books falling over. Sadly, you don't get to see all of them in the film.'

Much like Hermione's bag, these pasties are loaded with more filling than expected. Packed with a fragrant potato-based filling dotted with salty bacon, bright peas and sweet onions, they make a great snack that's healthy and satisfying.

PASTRY

325g plain flour

1 teaspoon coarse salt

115g very cold unsalted butter

50g very cold solid vegetable fat

90ml ice water

Egg wash (1 egg whisked with 1 tablespoon water)

✴ **BEHIND THE MAGIC** ✴

Hermione packs medicinal items such as Essence of Dittany that come in handy when Ron is splinched while apparating. Emma Watson felt that Hermione kept a very calm head, 'considering the love of her life is bleeding to death!'

Line a baking sheet with baking paper.

TO MAKE THE PASTRY:

In a large mixing bowl, combine the flour and salt. Cut the butter and vegetable fat into small pieces. Using a pastry cutter or two forks, work the butter and fat into the flour mixture until all the pieces are pea sized or smaller.

Add the ice water a little at a time and use the pastry cutter to bring the pastry together. As the pastry forms, switch to your hands or a spatula, adding more water until the dough just makes a ball.

Working with half the pastry at a time, on a lightly floured surface, roll out the pastry to about 3mm thick. Cut out 10cm circles and repeat with the second half of the pastry until you have 16 circles. Transfer the circles to the prepared baking sheet and chill in the refrigerator while you make the filling.

Continued on page 25

Continued from page 22

FILLING

- 115g Maris Piper potatoes, cut into 5mm dice
- 4 rashers bacon, chopped into 5mm strips
- 1 small brown onion, diced
- 2 tablespoons frozen peas
- ¼ teaspoon cumin
- ¼ teaspoon turmeric
- ¼ teaspoon cayenne
- Salt
- Pepper

TO MAKE THE FILLING:

In a small saucepan, bring salted water to the boil, add the potatoes and boil until tender over a medium-high heat, 12 to 15 minutes. Remove from the heat and drain. Transfer the potatoes to a large mixing bowl.

In a large frying pan over a medium heat, brown the bacon. Remove from the heat and add to the bowl with the potatoes. Add the onion to the frying pan; cook, stirring occasionally, until translucent, about 5 minutes. Add the peas, cumin, turmeric, cayenne, salt and pepper to the frying pan and stir well. Cook for 4–5 minutes until the peas are hot. Stir in the potatoes and bacon, remove from the heat and transfer to a bowl to cool for about 15 minutes. While the filling is cooling, preheat the oven to 200°C/180°C fan/Gas Mark 6.

Place 1 heaped tablespoon of filling into the centre of 8 of the circles, brush the edges with egg wash and cover with a second circle. Press firmly at the edges, or crimp with a fork, to seal. Transfer the sealed pasties to the prepared baking sheet and brush the tops with the remaining egg wash. Cut a small slit in the top of each pie. Place the baking sheet in the oven and bake for 25–30 minutes until golden.

> 'HOW THE RUDDY - ?'
> 'UNDETECTABLE EXTENSION CHARM.'
> 'YOU'RE AMAZING. YOU ARE.'
> 'ALWAYS THE TONE OF SURPRISE.'
>
> – Ron Weasley and Hermione Granger, *Harry Potter and the Deathly Hallows – Part 1*

THE BURROW
CURRANT SCONES

V | YIELD: 10 scones | PREP TIME: 15 minutes | COOK TIME: 20 minutes

In *Harry Potter and the Chamber of Secrets*, Fred, George and Ron Weasley fly Harry away from his imprisonment at Number Four, Privet Drive, in their father's enchanted car. They land safely at the Weasley home, The Burrow, in the early hours of the morning. After entering the house, a plate of goodies on the kitchen table is fair game for the growing boys to have an early nibble.

'Although The Burrow is whimsical, quirky and filled with magical things,' says director Chris Columbus, 'I also wanted it to feel like a warm family home: a place where Harry could feel very comfortable.'

These yummy scones reflect the comfort of the Weasley home. This recipe makes a wetter scone dough – firmer than muffins – and yields a tender baked good that's filled with dried currants (or blueberries, if you prefer), complemented with the flavours of almond and cinnamon.

100g dried dried currants

250g plain flour, plus more
  for rolling

1 tablespoon baking powder

50g sugar

½ teaspoon salt

85g cold unsalted butter,
  cut into pieces

1 medium egg

125ml milk

½ teaspoon almond extract

FOR SERVING

Butter

Jam

Clotted cream

Preheat the oven to 220°C/200°C fan/Gas Mark 7. Line a baking sheet with baking paper. In a heat-proof jug or bowl, cover the dried currants with boiling water, leave to stand for 30 minutes and drain (see note).

In a large bowl, sift together the flour, baking powder, sugar and salt. Add the butter and use two knives or a pastry cutter to cut it into the mixture. Fold in the dried currants.

In a small bowl, whisk together the egg, milk and almond extract. Add this to the flour mixture and fold together until all the dough is moist. Reserve the egg and milk bowl to use for an egg wash (do not rinse the bowl).

Turn out the dough on to a lightly floured surface, dust with more flour and gently roll into a 2.5cm-thick circle. Use a 5cm biscuit cutter to cut out as many scones as you can and transfer them to the prepared baking sheet. Gently form together the trimmings with your hands, keeping the thickness to 2.5cm and cut out a few more scones.

Splash a bit more milk into the egg-and-milk bowl, stir to combine the milk with egg remnants and use a pastry brush to brush the tops of each scone.

Place the baking sheet in the oven and bake for 12–15 minutes or until the scones are golden on the tops and edges. Leave to cool for a few minutes before serving. Serve with butter, jam and clotted cream.

NOTE

Soaking the dried currants is an extra step, but worth it: the dried currants become tender and delicious bites, and because they are hydrated, they don't draw moisture from the scones during baking.

'DO YOU THINK IT WOULD BE ALL RIGHT
IF WE HAD SOME OF THIS?'
'YEAH. MUM WILL NEVER KNOW.'

– Ron and George Weasley, *Harry Potter and the Chamber of Secrets*

ORDER OF THE PHOENIX CITRUS BREAD

✷

V | YIELD: 1 loaf | PREP TIME: 2 hours 20 minutes | COOK TIME: 35 minutes

---

In *Harry Potter and the Order of the Phoenix*, Harry's first official meeting with the members of the Order of the Phoenix takes place at Number Twelve, Grimmauld Place, which is Sirius Black's ancestral seat. Among other members, the Order includes Mr and Mrs Weasley, Nymphadora Tonks and two of Harry's professors: Remus Lupin and Alastor Moody. They gather in the kitchen of Grimmauld Place to discuss the dangerous political climate.

Four-metre-high sideboards are jammed with old silverware and pewter in a jumbled mess because the elderly house-elf Kreacher is looking after the house. A collection of dark blue-and-gold-rimmed china is imprinted with the family crest, designed by the graphics department.

This round risen bread loaf with a smaller round loaf on top looks just like the one Mrs Weasley has set out for their meal. There is a hint of sweetness from the sugar and orange juice, a slight citrus aroma from the orange and lime zests and a crisp crust. It is delightful toasted with butter.

- 475g strong white flour
- 1 teaspoon coarse salt
- 65g caster sugar
- 2¼ teaspoons fast-action dried yeast
- 55g unsalted butter, diced, plus more for greasing
- 90ml fresh orange juice
- Zest of 1 orange
- 60ml lime juice
- Zest of 1 lime
- 150ml warm water
- 1 egg, beaten

Sift the flour, salt, sugar and dried yeast together in the bowl of a stand mixer or a large mixing bowl if using a hand mixer. Add the butter and use a pastry cutter or two knives to cut the butter into the flour mixture.

Add the orange juice, orange zest, lime juice, lime zest and warm water to the bowl. Using the dough hook, mix the dough until a cohesive ball forms, about 5 minutes. Grease a large bowl, transfer the dough to the bowl and cover; leave the dough to rise in a warm, draught-free place for about 1 hour or until it has doubled in size.

Line a baking sheet with baking paper. Divide the dough into 2 balls, one using two-thirds of the dough and the other using one-thrd of the dough. Place the larger ball on the prepared baking sheet and top with the smaller ball. Press a clean finger coated in flour into the centre of the smaller ball of dough. Cover with a towel and leave to rise for 1 hour.

Preheat the oven to 220°C/200°C fan/Gas Mark 7. Brush the dough with the beaten egg.

Bake for 30–35 minutes until golden. Remove from the oven and transfer the bread to a wire rack. Cool completely before slicing.

'THE ORDER OF THE PHOENIX.
IT'S A SECRET SOCIETY. DUMBLEDORE FORMED IT
WHEN THEY FIRST FOUGHT YOU-KNOW-WHO.'

– Hermione Granger, *Harry Potter and the Order of the Phoenix*

DUDLEY'S SPECIAL DAY BREAKFAST

GF* | YIELD: 4 servings | PREP TIME: 10 minutes | COOK TIME: 40 minutes

It's Dudley Dursley's eleventh birthday! When he arrives in the kitchen on this special day, Dudley's mother, Petunia, snaps at her nephew, Harry, to cook breakfast. Dudley's father, Vernon, barks at Harry to get his coffee.

The Dursley residence 'is not particularly tasteful,' says production designer Stuart Craig. Set decorator Stephenie McMillan channelled what she thought would be Petunia's particular design aesthetic. 'We looked for the ugliest sofas, the worst tiles for the kitchen, the shiniest, most horrible fireplace,' she said, and the furniture needed to be in 'really nasty colours'.

This traditional English breakfast includes roasted tomato, roasted mushrooms, fried eggs, beans, sausage and rashers of bacon. It is a hearty meal that is certainly filling and exploding with flavour. Nothing but the best for Dudley.

8 rashers back bacon

4 sausages or 8 chippolatas

3 tablespoons olive oil

200g button mushrooms, cleaned and stalks removed

Salt

Pepper

4 small tomatoes, halved

8 medium eggs

4 slices sourdough bread

Butter, for toast

2 cans vegetarian beans or baked beans

Preheat the oven to its lowest setting. Line a baking sheet with foil and place it in the oven.

Heat 1 tablespoon olive oil in a large frying pan over a medium heat, then add the sausages. Fry 12–15 minutes, turning often to brown evenly, until cooked through. About halfway through, add the bacon to the pan and cook for 5–7 minutes, turning once. Transfer the cooked meat to the baking sheet in the oven.

Add 1 tablespoon olive oil to the frying pan and fry the mushrooms until browned, 5–7 minutes. Season with salt and pepper while cooking. Once done, transfer to the baking sheet in the oven.

Season the cut-side of the tomatoes with salt and pepper. Place cut-side-down in the frying pan and cook for 2–3 minutes until warmed. Transfer to the baking sheet in the oven, with the cut-side facing up.

Wipe out the frying pan with damp kitchen paper. Add the remaining 1 tablespoon olive oil. Cook the eggs, 1–2 at a time, until the white is set but the yolk remains runny. Transfer to a plate and continue until all the eggs have been cooked.

While the eggs are cooking, toast and butter the bread. Divide the bacon, sausage, mushrooms, tomatoes and bread among four plates.

Heat the beans in a medium saucepan over a medium heat until steamy, 4–5 minutes. Serve on the plates or in small bowls. Enjoy immediately.

NOTE

This recipe is easily made gluten-free by using gluten-free bread

'I WANT EVERYTHING TO BE PERFECT FOR MY DUDLEY'S SPECIAL DAY.'

– Petunia Dursley, *Harry Potter and the Philosopher's Stone*

DIAGON ALLEY
STEAK AND ALE PIE

✳

YIELD: 6 servings | PREP TIME: 30 minutes | COOK TIME: 2 hours

Diagon Alley exemplifies the ubiquitous shopping alleyways found around London that host shops, pubs and eateries. Hoping for a Dickensian design of Diagon Alley, filmmakers looked around the city for a practical place to shoot, but few fit the bill. 'There would always be something modern there like a phone booth or grocery store,' says *Harry Potter and the Philosopher's Stone* director Chris Columbus. 'We could have tried to work around those, but we realized it would be best to build a set.' Creating Diagon Alley in the studio proved advantageous. 'We wanted crumbling, ancient dereliction,' says production designer Stuart Craig. 'Nothing too smart or done up. It's as full of character as we could possibly make it.'

Steak and Ale Pie, much like the Steak and Kidney Pie offered at The Leaky Cauldron, encases a steak and ale mixture, along with carrots and onions, in a pastry in this classic British pub fare.

FILLING

450g beef braising steak, cut into 1cm cubes

2 tablespoons plain flour

1 teaspoon salt

½ teaspoon pepper

1 tablespoon rapeseed oil

1 medium onion, diced

2 medium carrots, diced

115g mushrooms, sliced

2 garlic cloves, peeled and very finely chopped

2 tablespoons tomato purée

2 tablespoons Worcestershire sauce

350ml dark ale or stout beer

1 tablespoon chopped fresh thyme

1 tablespoon chopped fresh rosemary

TO MAKE THE FILLING:

In a large mixing bowl, toss the beef steak cubes with the flour, salt and pepper. Add the oil to a pot with a tightly fitting lid and heat over a medium heat.

Working in batches, brown the meat in the pot (don't overcrowd it), turning to ensure that all sides are seared. As it browns, transfer the meat from the pot to a bowl; continue until all the meat has been browned, then set aside.

Add the onions, carrots and mushrooms to the pot. Cook for 5–7 minutes or until softened. Add the garlic, tomato purée and Worcestershire sauce. Stir well and cook for 2–3 minutes.

Add the ale or beer to the pot and stir until combined. Leave to bubble for 2 minutes, then stir in the thyme, rosemary and browned beef. Cover, reduce heat to low and simmer for 30 minutes. Uncover, stir and simmer a further 15–20 minutes to reduce the gravy. Once the gravy coats the back of a spoon, remove from the heat and set aside.

Continued on page 34

Continued on page 34

Continued from page 33

PASTRY

55g salted butter, plus more for greasing the pan

500g plain flour, plus more for work surface

100g vegetable fat

60ml milk for glazing the pie

SPECIALIST TOOLS

20cm springform tin

✳ ─ NOTE ─────────

This pie can be served warm, at room temperature or chilled. To serve chilled, allow to cool for 2 hours, in the springform pan, at room temperature; then refrigerate overnight. Leftovers can be stored in an airtight container for up to 4 days.

✳ **BEHIND THE MAGIC** ✳

Production designer Stuart Craig wanted the buildings of Diagon Alley to have a 'gravity-defying lean' that emulated Dickensian architecture.

TO MAKE THE PASTRY:

Preheat the oven to 180°C/160°C fan/Gas Mark 4. Grease the springform tin well, ensuring to get in between the base and the sides. Place on a rimmed baking sheet and set aside. Add the flour to a large mixing bowl and use a wooden spoon to make a well in the centre; set aside.

In a small saucepan over a medium-high heat, add 175ml water, the vegetable fat and the butter. Stir until the fat and butter are melted and the mixture begins to boil. Add the mixture to the well in the flour and use the wooden spoon to stir it until it is cool enough to handle, about 2 minutes. Knead the mixture a bit until all the ingredients are incorporated.

Remove two-thirds of the dough to a lightly floured surface, covering the remaining dough with a tea towel and roll it out to about a 5mm thickness. Gently lift the dough into the springform tin, making sure it is all the way to the base and pressed against the sides. If any tears occur, patch by pressing the dough back together or adding trimmings to fill in. Trim the edges so there is about a 1cm overhang all the way around the edges.

Work the trimmings and the remaining pastry back together and roll out to about 5mm thick to make the top. Fill the springform tin with the steak filling and make smooth. Using a pastry brush, brush the edges of the pastry with milk; lay the pastry top over the filling. Trim the pastry top to a matching 1cm overhang and press the two pastry edges together; ensure the pastry is sealed well and crimp as desired. Brush the entire top with milk.

Place the pie in the oven and bake for 45–50 minutes or until golden. Remove from the oven and cool for at least 20 minutes before serving. To serve, place the springform tin on a chopping board, unclip the clasp to open and remove the side. If desired, use a bench scraper or offset spatula to gently remove the pie from the base of the tin and slide it on to the chopping board. Slice and serve.

'THIS ESTABLISHMENT OF DIAGON ALLEY – THE LEAKY CAULDRON – WILL TODAY BE SERVING THE FOLLOWING SPECIALTIES…'

– Sign in The Leaky Cauldron, *Harry Potter and the Philosopher's Stone*

LUCHINO CAFFE PICANTE PANINIS

✳

GF* | YIELD: 4 servings | PREP TIME: 10 minutes | COOK TIME: 35 minutes

Harry, Ron and Hermione Apparate to Shaftesbury Avenue in Piccadilly Circus after hearing that the Ministry of Magic has fallen. They quickly hide in a coffee shop off Tottenham Road – the Luchino Caffe – to work out what to do next.

The Luchino Caffe was created for *Harry Potter and the Deathly Hallows – Part 1* and named after the son of graphic designer Miraphora Mina. The graphics artists frequently used the names of friends and family to supplement whatever they did not glean from the books. The Luchino Caffe also offers a Lima Lush citrus crush fizzy drink, named after graphics artist Eduardo Lima.

This panini is inspired by the Picante Panini on the menu. Spicy sausage slices are a nice contrast to this panini's sweet roasted red peppers and crisp, thin onions add a texture contrast to the provolone cheese (or edam if you cannot find it) and other fillings. These satisfying sandwiches work for lunch or dinner.

- 450g spicy Italian sausages
- 8 slices sourdough bread
- 8 slices provolone cheese or edam cheese
- 60g roasted red peppers, sliced
- 4 thin slices red onions
- 1 tablespoon olive oil

Preheat the oven to 190°C/170°C fan/Gas Mark 5. Line a baking sheet with foil. Place the sausages on the prepared baking sheet and bake, turning occasionally, for 20–25 minutes until cooked through. Remove from the oven and slice into 5mm-thick rounds.

On 4 slices of the bread, place 1 slice of provolone cheese or edam cheese each. Top with sliced sausage to cover and then place one-quarter of the roasted red peppers and red onions. Place a slice of cheese on each and top with another slice of bread.

Heat a panini press (or a large frying pan and a foil-covered brick) over a medium heat. Once hot, brush with olive oil. Cook each sandwich, pressing with the panini press or brick, until hot and golden, 8–10 minutes.

Leave to cool for 2–3 minutes; cut each sandwich in half and serve.

✳ **BEHIND THE MAGIC** ✳

The scene in Shaftesbury Avenue was shot on a very cold night. Daniel Radcliffe and Rupert Grint could wear thermals under their costumes, but Emma Watson could not. 'I don't imagine it's an overly pleasant feeling to be cold and shivering at 3 am,' says Radcliffe. 'I felt quite sorry for Emma.'

'LOCK THE DOOR. GET THE LIGHTS.'
– Harry Potter, *Harry Potter and the Deathly Hallows – Part 1*

✳ NOTE

This recipe is easily made gluten-free by using gluten-free bread

ALL BETTER NOW CHOCOLATE CAKES

V | YIELD: 12 cakes | PREP TIME: 15 minutes | COOK TIME: 35 minutes

---

Chocolate in the wizarding world isn't just for a snack or dessert – it's actually good for you after a Dementor encounter, which Harry learns when Professor Remus Lupin offers him this remedy after a confrontation with these Dark creatures on the Hogwarts Express in *Harry Potter and the Prisoner of Azkaban*.

Daniel Radcliffe (Harry) sees his character's encounter with the Dementor as a turning point. 'He developed this image in his own mind of him being this all-powerful wizard. He's defeated Voldemort twice, and he's getting more confident about his powers,' he explains. 'But then he faints when he sees the Dementor. It acts as a wakeup call to realize he does have weaknesses, he's not that powerful or that strong.' Naturally, Harry is not going to let that defeat him.

These lush individual dark chocolate cakes are dusted with cocoa powder and baked in special mini cake tins in the shape of a skull, the only visible body part of a Dementor.

Butter or oil, for greasing

250g plain flour

85g cocoa powder

1 tablespoon baking powder

1 teaspoon coarse salt

350g unsalted butter, softened

200g caster sugar

150g soft light brown sugar

4 medium eggs

1 tablespoon vanilla extract

175ml milk

85g mini chocolate chips

2 teaspoons icing sugar

2 teaspoons cocoa powder

SPECIALIST TOOLS

30 x 25cm skull cake tin with six 5cm-deep holes

Preheat the oven to 160°C/140°C fan/Gas Mark 3. Grease the insides of the skull cake tin.

In a large mixing bowl, sift together the flour, cocoa powder, baking powder and salt.

In the bowl of a stand mixer, or a separate large bowl if using a hand mixer, cream together the butter, caster sugar and brown sugar until smooth and light brown, 2–3 minutes. Add the eggs one at a time, mixing well after each addition.

Stir the vanilla extract with the milk in a small jug. With the mixer running on its lowest setting, alternate between adding the milk mixture and flour mixture to the butter mixture until all has been added. Scrape down the sides of the bowl as needed to ensure even mixing. Add the mini chocolate chips and blend to combine.

Fill each cavity about three-quarters full, tapping the tin to evenly distribute the mixture. Bake for 30–35 minutes until cooked through.

Cool for 10 minutes, then invert on to a wire rack (some cakes may need a little loosening at the edges to come out).

Sift together the icing sugar and cocoa powder in a small bowl. While still warm, dust the tops of the skull cakes with the mixture.

'HERE. EAT THIS. IT'LL HELP.
IT'S ALL RIGHT – IT'S CHOCOLATE.'

– Remus Lupin, *Harry Potter and the Prisoner of Azkaban*

SURBITON SMOKED HAM TOASTIES

GF* | YIELD: 4 servings | PREP TIME: 5 minutes | COOK TIME: 10 minutes

Harry Potter spends his time riding around on the trains of the London Underground over the summer in *Harry Potter and the Half-Blood Prince*. As he tells Dumbledore, '[It] takes my mind off things.' Harry also has been flirting with a waitress in a café at Surbiton Station, who noticed a moving picture in an issue of *The Daily Prophet* he'd been reading.

Those moving photographs in *The Daily Prophet* were created by the graphics department, who initially included a sketch suggesting what the visual should be. 'We'd send it in for approval,' says graphics artist Eduardo Lima, 'but the response would be, "That's good, but you know, it's not the image we'll be using."' The artists then simply wrote 'Moving Picture to Be Added Later' in the picture box for the visual effects team.

This toasted sandwich, inspired by items on the Surbiton Station menu, features smoked Gouda cheese, smoked ham and fig jam.

- 8 slices sourdough bread
- 40g salted butter, softened
- 2 tablespoons fig jam
- 8 slices (about 225g in total) smoked Gouda cheese
- 225g smoked ham, thinly sliced

Spread one side of each slice of bread with butter. On the unbuttered side of 4 slices, spread ½ tablespoon of fig jam on each. Top with a slice of smoked Gouda cheese and drape 55g of smoked ham on each. Top with another slice of Gouda and a slice of bread, with the butter-side out.

Heat a large frying pan over a medium-low heat. Add the sandwiches (you may need to cook 1 or 2 at a time) and cook, flipping once, until golden on both sides, 4–6 minutes per side.

Transfer to a chopping board and leave to cool for 2 minutes before slicing in half and serving.

✳ **BEHIND THE MAGIC** ✳

The final printed version of *The Daily Prophet* that appears in the films placed green-screen material where the moving images would be before their digital addition.

'HARRY POTTER. WHO'S HARRY POTTER?'
'OH. NO ONE. BIT OF A TOSSER, REALLY.'

– Surbiton Station Waitress and Harry Potter,
Harry Potter and the Half-Blood Prince

✳ **NOTE**

This recipe is easily made gluten-free by using gluten-free bread

THE BURROW
MEAT SLICES

***

YIELD: 8 servings | PREP TIME: 20 minutes | COOK TIME: 1 hour

***

'The Burrow has a crooked quality,' says Chris Columbus, director of *Harry Potter and the Chamber of Secrets*. 'The floors, the ceilings, the staircase – everything is a little slanted; nothing is really perfect.' Inside, the Weasley home is filled with whimsical magical objects: a frying pan washes itself, and two knitting needles knit a jumper by themselves. Prop makers also produced a fanciful clock with hands indicating where all the members of the family are at any given moment. Mark Williams (Arthur Weasley) remembers how taken everyone was by these artefacts. 'Even the grown-up actors had to be told, "Don't touch the props!"' he remembers. 'Stop poking around! Leave them alone!'

Julie Walters, who plays mum Molly Weasley, calls The Burrow 'gorgeous and homey. It's not about appearances or ambition; it's about love and protection and care, and that's why the Weasleys are so special.'

This handheld pie is special as well, stuffed with seasoned meat, onions and carrots and then wrapped in puff pastry. It's the perfect home-cooked meal to share at The Burrow or your own home.

- 1 large onion, cut into chunks
- 1 large carrot, cut into chunks
- 2 tablespoons Worcestershire sauce
- 1 large potato, grated
- 450g beef mince
- 1 teaspoon coarse salt
- ½ teaspoon pepper
- 2 sheets frozen puff pastry, thawed
- 1 medium egg, beaten

Preheat the oven to 190°C/170°C fan/Gas Mark 5. Line a baking sheet with baking paper.

In a small food processor, combine the onion, carrot and Worcestershire sauce and process until puréed.

In a large mixing bowl, add the onion mixture, potato, beef, salt and pepper. Mix together (use clean hands if needed) to fully combine.

Lay 1 puff pastry sheet on the prepared baking sheet. Top with the beef mince mixture. Pat into a single, even layer with a rubber spatula. Top with the second sheet of puff pastry. Brush with the beaten egg, discarding the excess.

Place the baking sheet in the oven and bake for 45–50 minutes or until golden. Remove from the oven and leave to cool for 10 minutes before slicing into squares.

'IT'S NOT MUCH, BUT IT'S HOME.'
'I THINK IT'S BRILLIANT.'

– Ron Weasley and Harry Potter, *Harry Potter and the Chamber of Secrets*

OWL POST CHICKEN PARCELS

YIELD: 4 servings | PREP TIME: 15 minutes | COOK TIME: 45 minutes

Owl Post, the mail-delivery service for the wizarding world, serves witches and wizards throughout the world. At Hogwarts, the Owl Post brings *The Daily Prophet* newspapers, letters and parcels from home. But not all deliveries are eagerly received: Neville Longbottom receives a Remembrall from his grandmother in *Harry Potter and the Philosopher's Stone*. Ron Weasley's mother sends him a Howler in *Harry Potter and the Chamber of Secrets* that loudly chastises him in front of his peers.

The owls trained for the Owl Post did not actually carry the parcels and letters in their talons: the props were tied to a light plastic harness placed over the bird's body. The harness had a release mechanism attached to a long invisible cord held out of sight by a trainer. The owl flew towards a specific mark; then at a precise moment, the trainer pulled the wire to make the parcel fall.

This crisp, buttery puff pastry is filled with fried leeks, vibrant garlic, earthy herbs and meaty chicken and then topped with more leeks. Any Hogwarts students would be more than thrilled to receive this flavourful parcel from the Owl Post.

450g chicken breasts, pounded thin and cut into 4 pieces

Salt

Pepper

1 tablespoon olive oil

30g unsalted butter

1 leek, thinly sliced

2 cloves garlic, very finely chopped

1 teaspoon very finely chopped fresh thyme

1 teaspoon very finely chopped fresh sage

1 sheet frozen puff pastry, defrosted and cut into 4 even rectangles

Preheat the oven to 200°C/180°C fan/Gas Mark 6. Line a baking sheet with baking paper.

Season the chicken breasts on both sides with salt and pepper.

Heat the olive oil in a large frying pan set over a medium heat. Add the chicken breasts, and cook, flipping once, until lightly browned on both sides, 5–6 minutes per side. Transfer the chicken to a plate.

Melt the butter in the frying pan. Add the leek and fry 10–12 minutes until tender. Add the garlic, thyme and sage, and stir well. Cook for 1–2 minutes. Season with salt and pepper, then remove from heat.

Set the 4 puff pastry rectangles on the prepared baking sheet. Top each with 1 chicken breast on the diagonal. Using half of the leek mixture, divide it evenly and spread it over each of the 4 chicken breasts. Reserve the remaining leek mixture. Pull 2 opposing puff pastry corners over the chicken and leeks to meet in the centre, using a bit of water on the points of the pastry to help it seal.

Bake for 25–30 minutes or until the puff pastry is golden.

Serve with the remaining leek mixture spooned over the top.

NOTE

Wash the leeks thoroughly, or you could end up with some sand in the dish.

'AH, MAIL'S HERE!'

– Ron Weasley, *Harry Potter and the Philosopher's Stone*

ARTHUR WEASLEY'S MUGGLE-INSPIRED BAKED GNOCCHI CASSEROLE

YIELD: 4 servings | PREP TIME: 10 minutes | COOK TIME: 25 minutes

---

Harry visits the Weasley family home, The Burrow, for the first time in *Harry Potter and the Chamber of Secrets*. He meets the patriarch of the family, Arthur, who works in the Ministry of Magic's Misuse of Muggle Artefacts Office. 'Dad loves Muggles,' Ron tells Harry. 'Thinks they're fascinating.'

Actor Mark Williams saw his character as 'an amateur scientist, as it were, in the best tradition of Victorian naturalists, where he's an expert in his own field.' Williams believes Arthur is 'underrated by flashier sorts. But he's fascinated by the Muggle world and the way it works.'

This recipe, an ode to Arthur Weasley's fascination with Muggles, is super easy to make. The sauce is creamy, like a vodka sauce without the vodka. The gnocchi is paired with a tomato sauce, combined with broccoli, artichoke hearts, Parmesan cheese and shallots and topped with provolone cheese (if you cannot find provolone, try mozzarella or Cheddar, sliced or grated). Baked to perfection, it is both light and filling.

- 450g gnocchi, cooked to packet instructions
- 150g broccoli florets
- 1 x 400g can quartered artichoke hearts
- 1 x 675g jar pasta sauce
- 125ml double cream
- 65g Parmesan cheese, freshly grated
- 4 slices provolone cheese or other cheese

Preheat the oven to 190°C/170°C fan/Gas Mark 5.

In an oven-safe round casserole, combine the cooked gnocchi, broccoli and artichoke hearts, stirring well to combine. In a large mixing bowl, stir together the pasta sauce, double cream and Parmesan cheese until combined. Pour the sauce over the gnocchi mixture and stir well. Top with the slices of provolone or other cheese.

Bake for 20–25 minutes or until the cheese is fully melted and the casserole is bubbly at the sides. Leave to cool 5 minutes before serving.

> 'NOW, HARRY, YOU MUST KNOW ALL ABOUT MUGGLES. TELL ME WHAT EXACTLY IS THE FUNCTION OF A RUBBER DUCK?'
>
> – Arthur Weasley, *Harry Potter and the Chamber of Secrets*

★ BEHIND THE MAGIC ★

To keep a look of surprise on Harry's face during each take of the breakfast scene, Williams asked Daniel Radcliffe a different question each time (not just about rubber ducks).

SHELL COTTAGE SEED BREAD

V | YIELD: 1 loaf | PREP TIME: 4 hours | COOK TIME: 40 minutes

Harry, Ron, Hermione and Luna, along with wandmaker Garrick Ollivander and Griphook the goblin, find refuge at Shell Cottage after they escape Malfoy Manor in *Harry Potter and the Deathly Hallows – Part 2*. The cottage, home of Bill and Fleur (née Delacour) Weasley, is just as it sounds: 'It's a little English cottage,' says production designer Stuart Craig, 'made out of extraordinary materials.' Three types of shells were used to suggest its whimsical yet credible construction. The walls are big oyster shells, the rooftop is covered in huge scallop shells and large razor shells create the ridge tiles.

As water boils on the hob, Bill sets out teacups for their guests on a small kitchen table that also holds a round loaf of seed bread. You would not know it to see it, but the loaf from this recipe is filled with sunflower seeds, linseeds and pumpkin seeds. It's perfect for toasting, with a yeasty goodness complemented by a knob or two of butter.

400g strong white flour, plus more for dusting

2 teaspoons fast-action dried yeast

35g roasted, salted sunflower seeds

70g roasted, salted pumpkin seeds

1 tablespoon linseed

1 tablespoon sesame seeds

2 teaspoons coarse salt

350ml warm water

2 tablespoons sugar

TOPPING

1 tablespoon roasted, salted pumpkin seeds

1 tablespoon roasted, salted sunflower seeds

½ teaspoon linseed

½ teaspoon sesame seeds

Sift together the flour and yeast in a large mixing bowl. Add the sunflower seeds, pumpkin seeds, linseed, sesame seeds and salt; mix. Whisk together the water and sugar in a small mixing bowl. Add to the flour mixture and mix until combined.

Shape the dough into a loaf inside the mixing bowl and cover with a tea towel. Leae to rise for 3 hours or until doubled in size.

Line a baking sheet with baking paper and dust with a little flour. Transfer the dough to the prepared baking sheet, handling it as little as possible. Press the topping seeds (pumpkin seeds, sunflower seeds, linseed and sesame seeds) into the dough all over. Cut an X into the centre, or go for a more decorative pattern. Cover with the tea towel and leave to rise for a further 45 minutes.

Preheat the oven to 220°C/200°C fan/Gas Mark 7. Place the baking sheet on the centre rack and bake for 35–40 minutes or until browned.

Leave to cool for 20 minutes before slicing.

> 'IT WAS OUR AUNT'S. WE USED TO COME HERE AS KIDS. THE ORDER USES IT NOW AS A SAFE HOUSE... WHAT'S LEFT OF US, AT LEAST.'
>
> – Bill Weasley, *Harry Potter and the Deathly Hallows – Part 2*

GINNY WEASLEY'S STAR SUGAR TARTLETS

✳

V | YIELD: 6 servings | PREP TIME: 20 minutes | COOK TIME: 35 minutes

During a Christmas break spent at The Burrow in *Harry Potter and the Half-Blood Prince*, Harry becomes closer to Ginny Weasley, who's been smitten with him since they met on Platform 9¾ many years before. Harry's attraction to her becomes more apparent with their every interaction, although he struggles to keep it a secret from her brother and his best friend, Ron.

'Harry's so close to the family,' admits Bonnie Wright, who plays the youngest Weasley. 'I saw it developing into a sister/brother relationship.'

During Christmas time at The Burrow, bowls of nuts and chocolates and plates of biscuits are set out for a sweet holiday. Ginny offers Harry another of the confections set out for guests and family: a small tart with a biscuit star on top. Her strategy seems to be working – until Ron shows up and sits uncomfortably in between them.

This miniature version of a brown sugar tart, with a vanilla butterscotch taste and covered with a bubbly bright star, will be sure to tempt any potential sweetheart.

3 tablespoons plain flour, plus more for work surface

1 recipe of 'The Ministry Is Watching' Pear Ginger Pastry (see page 106)

Egg wash, 1 egg plus 1 tablespoon of water

2 tablespoons gold sanding sugar or golden granulated sugar

30g butter, melted

125ml milk

325g soft light brown sugar

1 teaspoon vanilla extract

¼ teaspoon salt

2 medium eggs

SPECIALIST TOOLS
Mini star biscuit cutter

5cm star biscuit cutter (optional)

On a lightly floured surface roll out the pastry to 3mm thick. Cut the pastry into 12 rounds using a 10cm biscuit cutter. Cut 24 mini stars from the remaining pastry. Any extra pastry can be used to cut out the larger stars, if desired. Fit the rounds into 12 muffin tin holes and place the stars on a baking sheet. Chill both the muffin tin and the baking sheet for at least 30 minutes. Towards the end of the chilling preheat the oven to 190°C/170°C fan/Gas Mark 5.

When ready to bake, use a fork to prick the muffin tin pastries all over, being careful not to pierce all the way through. Bake for 10–15 minutes. While baking, prepare the egg wash by mixing the egg and water in a small bowl. Remove the muffin tin from the oven and brush all over with the egg wash. Brush each star with the egg wash and scatter with golden granulated sugar. Return the tart cases to the oven with the stars and bake for a further 7–10 minutes or until golden brown.

Towards the end of baking the tart cases, in a large bowl, whisk together the butter, flour, milk, brown sugar, vanilla extract and salt until well combined.

Continued on page 51

Continued from page 48

Continued from page 48

✶ BEHIND THE MAGIC ✶

'I was honestly quite oblivious to the fact that they would end up together,' admits Bonnie Wright.

In a small bowl, whisk the eggs. Add to the butter mixture and whisk to combine. Divide evenly among the 12 pastry cases. Lower the oven temperature to 140°C/120°C fan/Gas Mark 1.

Place the muffin tin into the oven and bake for 15–20 minutes or until the tartlets are puffed and golden. The edges should be firm, but it's okay if the centre is still a little jiggly.

Remove from the oven, top immediately with 2 mini stars each and cool 10 minutes in the muffin pan before transferring the tartlets to a cooling rack.

> 'OPEN UP, YOU.'
>
> – Ginny Weasley, *Harry Potter and the Half-Blood Prince*

BILL AND FLEUR'S WEDDING CHOCOLATE PUFFS

V | YIELD: 28–30 spirals | PREP TIME: 20 minutes | COOK TIME: 25 minutes

The wedding of the eldest Weasley sibling, Bill, to Triwizard champion Fleur Delacour in *Harry Potter and the Deathly Hallows – Part 1* is replete with sweetness and charm – especially in the confectionaries served at the reception. Among the spread are petit fours, tiny éclairs and strawberries dipped in chocolate, among others – almost all prepared out of silicone rubber.

'We did have some real food on the tables for people to be seen eating,' said set decorator Stephenie McMillan, who confessed that it took several tries to get the right size for the little pastries. 'Harry Potter usually has things larger than life, and we were first shown really big flans and huge fruit tarts. So I had to ask for another attempt.' Once achieved, the props department went to work, creating four thousand delicious-looking desserts.

Any occasion for enjoying these puffed pastry delicacies drizzled in chocolate is sure to be a celebration.

2 tablespoons soft light brown sugar

½ teaspoon ground ginger

¼ teaspoon ground cardamom

30g ground almonds

Flour, for the chopping board

1 sheet frozen puff pastry, defrosted

1 tablespoon unsalted butter, melted

55g dark chocolate (at least 70% cocoa)

55g white chocolate

Silver sanding sugar (optional)

Edible gold foil stars (optional)

Preheat the oven to 200°C/180°C fan/Gas Mark 6. Line a baking sheet with baking paper and set aside.

In a small bowl, mix together the brown sugar, ginger, cardamom and almonds and set aside.

Lightly flour a chopping board and lay out the defrosted puff pastry. It should be about 28 x 25cm; roll it out a bit, if necessary. Brush the surface of the pastry with the melted butter, then scatter with the brown sugar mixture.

To roll up the pastry, grasp a long side and roll it in, towards the other long side, in a tight spiral. Chill the roll for 20 minutes. Use a sharp knife to cut the rolled pastry into 1cm slices. Continue until all the pastry has been used.

Arrange the spirals on the prepared baking sheet. The spirals should not touch, but they can be placed less than 2.5cm apart. Place the baking sheet in the oven and bake for 15–20 minutes or until the spirals are lightly browned. Remove from the oven and cool completely.

Continued on page 55

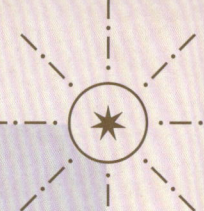

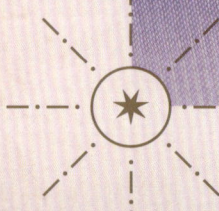

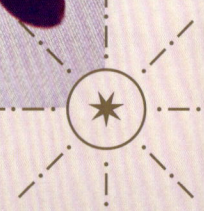

Continued from page 52

★ BEHIND THE MAGIC ★

The tiered trays holding the reception food were made from a material that would break safely when the wedding guests rushed out, knocking them over.

Once cool, break the dark chocolate and white chocolate into small pieces and place in separate microwave-safe bowls. Microwave separately for 30-second intervals, stirring after each one, until the chocolate is fully melted and smooth. Use a fork or small whisk to drizzle each pastry with first the dark chocolate, then the white chocolate. Scatter with sanding sugar and stars, if using. Leave to cool and harden completely.

Cool completely and store in an airtight container for up to 5 days.

'IT SEEMS SILLY, DOESN'T IT, A WEDDING?
GIVEN EVERYTHING THAT'S GOING ON.'
'MAYBE THAT'S THE BEST REASON TO HAVE IT,
BECAUSE OF EVERYTHING THAT'S GOING ON.'

– Ginny Weasley and Harry Potter, *Harry Potter and the Deathly Hallows – Part 1*

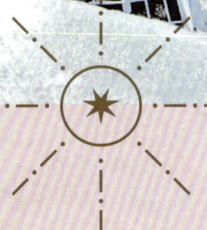

Chapter Two

HOGWARTS

Cedric Diggory

PROFESSOR SLUGHORN'S DINNER PARTY SAUSAGE ROLLS

✴

YIELD: 6 servings | PREP TIME: 25 minutes | COOK TIME: 25 minutes

When Potions Professor Horace Slughorn is persuaded to return to Hogwarts in *Harry Potter and the Half-Blood Prince*, he revives his practice of hosting parties with invitees that include interesting or celebrity-related students.

For these events, production designer Stuart Craig wanted Slughorn's office to be 'fairly substantial and very plush', so he overhauled the large set of the Room of Requirement. Set decorator Stephenie McMillan filled it with big leather Chesterfield sofas, a round table to seat thirteen people, a grand piano and a large desk. 'It has a certain sort of theatricality, doesn't it?' says Craig. 'Faded, bit threadbare, but, nonetheless, theatricality.' McMillan described it as 'sort of pompous, as Slughorn is.'

A traditional party nibble, this more sophisticated version of pigs in a blanket features seasoned sausage rolled into a log and wrapped in a light, airy puff pastry. After it's cut into bite-size pieces, it's baked to become a perfect party offering.

350g sausagemeat

1 teaspoon dried sage

1 teaspoon dried very finely chopped onion

1 teaspoon garlic powder

½ teaspoon coarse salt

1 sheet puff pastry, thawed

1 medium egg, beaten

Preheat the oven to 200°C/180°C fan/Gas Mark 6. Line a baking sheet with baking paper.

In a large mixing bowl, combine the sausagemeat, sage, onion, garlic powder and salt.

Cut the puff pastry into 4 equal strips and set them on a chopping board.

Divide the sausage mixture into 4 equal portions. One at a time, roll into logs the length of the puff pastry strips. Lay down the centre of one piece of puff pastry. Brush the edges of the puff pastry with the egg and fold around the sausage to seal. Cut into 11cm pieces and place on the prepared baking sheet about 2.5cm apart. Continue until all the logs have been formed and cut.

Brush the sausage rolls with the remaining egg wash.

Place the baking sheet in the oven and bake for 20–25 minutes or until the pastry is golden and the sausage is cooked through. Leave to cool for 10 minutes before serving.

✴ **BEHIND THE MAGIC** ✴

The Room of Requirement set that was transformed into Professor Slughorn's office also served as the Trophy Room in *Harry Potter and the Goblet of Fire*.

'IN THE OLD DAYS, I USED TO THROW TOGETHER THE OCCASIONAL SUPPER PARTY. SELECT STUDENT OR TWO. WOULD YOU BE GAME?'

– Horace Slughorn to Harry Potter, *Harry Potter and the Half-Blood Prince*

SLUG CLUB PRAWN AND CHORIZO SKEWERS

✶

YIELD: 4 servings | PREP TIME: 15 minutes | COOK TIME: 10 minutes

---

Prior to the Christmas break in *Harry Potter and the Half-Blood Prince*, Horace Slughorn hosts a holiday party bringing together current and former members of his Slug Club. The Potions professor gives a nod to the season by dressing his office in muted versions of traditional red and green holiday colours.

Creating the party's palette brought together the design and costume departments. 'This was certainly a case where departments influenced each other,' says production designer Stuart Craig. 'Jany Temime showed me the costume [Slughorn] would wear for the party, with its silver tassels. This complimented the party decorations and the lanterns. There's a sort of eccentricity to both that matches.'

Inspired by the appetizers served during Slughorn's holiday party, these skewers are basted with garlic oil and served on warm ciabatta bread. The spicy chorizo and meaty prawns are a luxurious match, and the companion garlic toast helps these reach all the right flavour and texture notes.

- 1 loaf ciabatta bread
- 1 tablespoon olive oil
- 1 clove garlic, very finely chopped
- Sea salt

VINAIGRETTE
- 1 shallot, peeled and very finely chopped
- 2 tablespoons lemon juice
- 1 tablespoon Dijon mustard
- 1 tablespoon honey
- 60ml olive oil
- ¼ teaspoon chilli flakes
- 1 teaspoon coarse salt
- ½ teaspoon pepper

- 450g cooked large prawns, peeled and deveined
- 55g sliced, dry-cured Ibérico chorizo

SPECIALIST TOOLS
- Twelve to sixteen 15cm skewers

Preheat the oven to 180°C/160°C fan/Gas Mark 4. Slice the bread thinly.

Heat the olive oil over a medium heat in a small frying pan. Add the garlic and cook until fragrant, about 1 minute. Remove from heat, and brush the garlic and oil on one side of the bread slices. Season lightly with sea salt, place on a baking sheet and place in the oven 3–5 minutes until toasted.

TO MAKE THE VINAIGRETTE:

In a small bowl, whisk together the shallot, lemon juice, mustard, honey, olive oil, chilli flakes, salt and pepper.

On the skewers, thread a prawn, then a piece of chorizo (fold it like an accordion) and a second prawn on each one. Using a pastry brush, brush the prawns with the vinaigrette and serve the extra alongside the bread and skewers.

> 'WAS I UNDER THE IMPRESSION THAT HE AND I WOULD BE ATTENDING PROFESSOR SLUGHORN'S CHRISTMAS PARTY TOGETHER? YES. NOW, GIVEN THE CIRCUMSTANCES, I'VE HAD TO MAKE OTHER ARRANGEMENTS.'
>
> – Hermione Granger, speaking about Ron Weasley, *Harry Potter and the Half-Blood Prince*

NIMBUS 2000 TOASTED PARMESAN BROOMS WITH PINE NUT ROASTED GARLIC HUMMUS

✳

YIELD: 24–26 brooms | PREP TIME: 1¾–2½ hours | COOK TIME: 25–35 minutes

---

When Harry Potter proves himself to be an exceptional broom flyer in *Harry Potter and the Philosopher's Stone* and earns a spot on the Gryffindor Quidditch team as the new Seeker – and the youngest Quidditch player in a century – he's gifted a Nimbus 2000 broom by Minerva McGonagall, the Gryffindor Head of House. It is the fastest model out there.

On set, each broom had a bicycle seat bolted on that was covered by the player's robes while flying, along with a set of visible foot pedals to cradle the actor's legs. 'The filmmakers wanted the actors to ride the brooms like jockeys, with their feet tucked underneath,' explains prop model Pierre Bohanna.

In this recipe, a focaccia flavoured with Parmesan cheese is cut into long, thin pieces and shaped to create a broom-like design; then it is served with homemade hummus flavoured with pine nuts and roasted garlic. You will be flying high with this tasty snack.

BREAD BROOMS
350ml warm water (not over 43°C)

1 teaspoon sugar

1 tablespoon coarse salt, plus extra for seasoning

2¼ teaspoons fast-action dried yeast

550g strong white flour

75g Parmesan cheese, freshly grated

1 teaspoon garlic powder

60ml olive oil

1 tablespoon mixed poppy seeds and sesame seeds (optional)

1 teaspoon dried rosemary (optional)

2 tablespoons balsamic vinegar (optional)

TO MAKE THE BREAD BROOMS:
In the bowl of a stand mixer or a large mixing bowl if using a hand-held mixer, add the water, sugar and salt; stir gently to combine. Scatter the yeast over the top and leave to stand for 2–3 minutes or until foamy. Add the flour, 60g of the Parmesan and the garlic powder. Stir on low with a dough hook until the dough comes together. The dough should still be slightly sticky.

Use 1 tablespoon olive oil to grease the inside of a large bowl. Add the dough and give it 1–2 turns to coat with the oil. Cover the bowl loosely with a tea towel and place it in a warm spot for 1 hour or until the dough has doubled in size and is puffy.

Grease both baking sheets with 1 tablespoon of olive oil each. One sheet at a time, turn out the dough on to the baking sheet and begin to stretch it to fill the sheet. If it resists stretching, leave it to rest, covered with the tea towel, 5 minutes at a time until it easily stretches to fill the pan.

Once the dough is stretched to fill the pan, use a greased knife or pizza wheel to cut it into 2.5cm strips lengthways. You should get 12–13 strips; this does not have to be an exact measurement. Now cut all the strips in half across the middle, doubling the number of strips.

Continued on page 69

Continued from page 66

HUMMUS

1 head garlic

50ml olive oil

1 x 400g can chickpeas, drained and rinsed

2 tablespoons toasted sesame seeds

60ml lemon juice

½ teaspoon salt

¼ teaspoon pepper

35g pine nuts, toasted

SPECIALIST TOOLS

Two 46 x 33cm rimmed baking sheets

Working with the second oiled baking sheet and one strip at a time, create the brooms by picking up a strip, twisting it for almost the whole length and flattening one end. The flattened end should be 2.5–5cm. Lay the strip on the baking sheet and repeat until all the strips have been shaped. Brush each bread broom with the remaining olive oil, cover and leave to rise for 45–60 minutes until puffy. The brooms will not rise much during this time. Towards the end of this rise, preheat the oven to 180°C/160°C fan/Gas Mark 4.

Using the pizza wheel or a paring knife, cut each flattened end into 5–6 strips (there is no need to separate them), then pinch the bottom ends together to create the rounded broom bristles.

Scatter the bristles with the mixed seeds and a bit of rosemary, if using, and season with salt to taste. If using, brush balsamic vinegar on the handles and scatter them with the remaining 2 tablespoons Parmesan. Bake for 25–30 minutes or until golden brown.

TO MAKE THE HUMMUS:

Preheat the oven to 200°C/180°C fan/Gas Mark 6. Cut the top 5mm off the garlic head for the hummus. Drizzle the garlic with 1 teaspoon of olive oil and wrap it fully in foil. Cook it in the oven for 1 hour.

Carefully unwrap the roasted garlic head and squeeze the cloves into a food processor. Add the chickpeas, toasted sesame seeds, lemon juice, 3 tablespoons olive oil, salt, pepper and 2 tablespoons toasted pine nuts. Process until smooth. Transfer to a bowl and scatter with the remaining pine nuts. These are delightful served with the brooms and/or fresh seasonal vegetables for dipping.

✳ BEHIND THE MAGIC ✳

Multiple brooms were purchased secretly for the shops and classes in *Philosopher's Stone*. One crew member told a shopkeeper she was buying so many brooms because she had a lot of sweeping to do.

> **'THAT'S NOT JUST A BROOMSTICK, HARRY. IT'S A NIMBUS 2000!'**
>
> – Ron Weasley, *Harry Potter and the Philosopher's Stone*

ROOM OF REQUIREMENT MEATBALLS IN RED WINE SAUCE

✦

YIELD: 4 servings | PREP TIME: 20 minutes | COOK TIME: 30 minutes

Hermione Granger spearheads Dumbledore's Army (DA): a secret student organization created when their Defence Against the Dark Arts professor, Dolores Umbridge, refuses to teach defensive magic in *Harry Potter and the Order of the Phoenix*. Harry is appointed as the instructor, but where can they practise? Neville Longbottom finds the Room of Requirement, which becomes the DA's headquarters.

'In the book, the room was "cushiony", with cushions and bookshelves filled with books,' says Matthew Lewis (Neville). 'But in the film, there's lots of mirrors everywhere and steel grills on the floor. It's a really atmospheric set that looks like an underground fight club in Hogwarts.'

Much like the Room of Requirement, these tender meatballs in a red wine sauce can be adapted to meet your purpose. Spoon them on rolls for a sandwich, serve them over mashed potatoes for a lovely comfort food, or layer them over noodles. They can even be served with cocktail sticks as an easy starter.

MEATBALLS

- 90g fresh breadcrumbs (2–3 slices sandwich bread)
- 3 tablespoons milk
- 450g beef mince
- 50g Parmesan cheese, freshly grated
- 1 medium egg, beaten
- 1 teaspoon dried thyme
- 1 teaspoon dried rosemary
- 1 teaspoon garlic powder
- 1 teaspoon paprika
- 1 teaspoon coarse salt
- ½ teaspoon pepper

> ✶ **NOTE**
> To make fresh breadcrumbs, add the bread to a food processor and pulse until it's reduced to fine crumbs.

TO MAKE THE MEATBALLS:

Preheat the oven to 200°C/180°C fan/Gas Mark 6.

In a large mixing bowl, thoroughly combine the breadcrumbs, milk, beef mince, Parmesan, egg, thyme, rosemary, garlic powder, paprika, salt and pepper. Break off pieces of the meat mixture and roll into 2.5cm meatballs. Arrange in a 33 x23cm rectangular ceramic dish. The meatballs can be close to each other but should not touch. Continue until all the meat has been used.

Place the dish in the oven and bake for 20–25 minutes until the meatballs are cooked through. If you are uncertain, cut into one of the meatballs to be sure there is no pink inside.

Continued on page 73

MAINS

70

Continued from page 70

SAUCE

2 tablespoons olive oil

2 cloves garlic, very finely chopped

1 small onion, finely diced

2 tablespoons tomato purée

250ml red wine

125 beef stock

800g passata

Salt

Pepper

TO MAKE THE SAUCE:

Heat the olive oil in a 4-litre (or slightly larger) casserole set over a medium heat. Add the garlic and onion and cook, stirring occasionally, until softened, 10–12 minutes. Add the tomato purée, red wine, beef stock and passata. Stir well. Season with a little salt and pepper. Cover, reduce the heat to medium-low and simmer for 10 minutes. Uncover, stir and adjust the seasonings as needed.

Add the meatballs to the sauce and stir. Cook for a further 5 minutes. Remove from heat and serve. These can be enjoyed as an starter (serve with cocktail sticks, for easy grabbing), on rolls for a sandwich, over pasta, or sliced on bread, with extra bread for dipping in the sauce. They also can be spooned on to a salad, for a different take.

'THE ROOM OF REQUIREMENT ONLY APPEARS WHEN A PERSON HAS REAL NEED OF IT. AND IS ALWAYS EQUIPPED WITH THE SEEKER'S NEEDS.'

– Hermione Granger, *Harry Potter and the Order of the Phoenix*

VANISHING CRISPY CAULIFLOWER AND LEEK FRITTERS

V | YIELD: 4 servings | PREP TIME: 15 minutes | COOK TIME: 40 minutes

---

Magical artefacts and spells in the wizarding world can make objects and people disappear. Harry Potter inherits an Invisibility Cloak from his father, gifted to him during his first year at Hogwarts, in *Harry Potter and the Philosopher's Stone*. To make Daniel Radcliffe 'invisible', one side of the cloak was made from green-screen material that he could flip over himself to 'vanish'.

Severus Snape used a vanishing spell during a wand duel exhibition in *Harry Potter and the Chamber of Secrets*. During a battle between Draco Malfoy and Harry, Draco casts a spell to bring forth a large snake. The reptile is too much of a threat to the students, so Snape casts Evanesca to vanish the reptile.

There is no need for a spell or an Invisibility Cloak to make these savoury fritters vanish – everyone will quickly eat them up. They are made with cauliflower, leeks and garlic and then fried to perfection. Serve them hot with a chilled sweet chilli dipping sauce and they will disappear before your eyes!

I small cauliflower, cut into small florets

I tablespoon olive oil

I leek, quartered and thinly sliced

I teaspoon salt

½ teaspoon pepper

60g plain flour

I clove garlic, very finely chopped

I medium egg, beaten

I tablespoon rapeseed oil

Sweet chilli sauce, chilled

Add the cauliflower florets to a large saucepan with about 2.5cm of water. Cover and boil over a medium-high heat for 8–10 minutes or until tender. Remove from heat and drain. Transfer the cauliflower florets to a large mixing bowl and mash thoroughly.

In a large frying pan, heat the olive oil over a medium heat. Add the leek and fry until softened and beginning to brown, 7–8 minutes. Add the leek to the mixing bowl with the mashed cauliflower.

Add the salt, pepper, flour and garlic to the mixing bowl. Stir well to combine. Add the egg and stir well. Tip: do this last so that you do not end up with scrambled eggs in your fritters!

Preheat the oven to 110°C/90°C/Gas Mark ¼. Heat the rapeseed oil in a large frying pan over medium heat. Drop in the cauliflower batter by the tablespoonful (a small biscuit scoop makes quick work of this). Use the back of a spoon to gently press each scoop into a patty. Fry 3–4 minutes per side or until golden. Transfer the fritters to a baking sheet in the oven to stay warm while you cook more in batches.

Serve hot with chilled sweet chile sauce for dipping.

BEHIND THE MAGIC

The Vanishing Cabinet Draco Malfoy repairs in *Harry Potter and the Half-Blood Prince* has a lock mechanism on it created by Mark Bullimore, who also provided locks for the vaults at Gringotts Bank in *Harry Potter and the Philosopher's Stone*.

'EVANESCA!'

– Severus Snape, *Harry Potter and the Chamber of Secrets*

GOBLET OF FIRE SCOTCH PANCAKES WITH WARM, BUTTERY MAPLE SYRUP

V | YIELD: 4 servings | PREP TIME: 45 minutes | COOK TIME: 35 minutes

---

Breakfast is considered the most important meal of the day, especially for the champions of the Triwizard Tournament. The breakfasts served in the Great Hall of Hogwarts feature racks of toast (some that float beside the tables), sausages, rashers and eggs of every style. There's also cereal: the two favourite brands are Cheeri Owls and Pixie Puffs, both distributed by Honeydukes and made with honey, molasses and pixie dust. Jugs of pumpkin juice and milk also abound, topped with a hog's head stopper. The graphics artists on set came up with marketing slogans, games for the cereal boxes and lists of ingredients for the packaged products.

Scotch pancakes, an old breakfast favourite across the country, where they are known by other names such as Welsh cakes, make a great start to any champion's day when served with warm, buttery maple syrup.

40g unsalted butter

185g plain flour

1¼ teaspoons baking powder

1¼ teaspoons bicarbonate of soda

1 teaspoon coarse salt

1 medium egg

2 tablespoons caster sugar

400ml buttermilk

1 teaspoon vanilla extract

FOR SERVING

250ml maple syrup

15g salted butter

Melt 30g butter in a small microwave-safe bowl by microwaving it in 20-second intervals, stirring after each one, until melted. Cool slightly.

In a large bowl, sift together the flour, baking powder, bicarbonate of soda and salt.

In a medium bowl, whisk together the egg and sugar until light yellow and frothy, about 2 minutes. Add the buttermilk, melted butter and vanilla extract and whisk well for about 30 seconds.

Make a well in the centre of the flour mixture and pour in the egg mixture. Stir until it just begins to incorporate; it will be lumpy. Cover the bowl with a tea towel and leave to rest for 30 minutes.

Preheat the oven to 160°C/140°C fan/Gas Mark 3. Line a baking sheet with foil and place it in the oven.

Heat a cast iron griddle or frying pan over a medium heat. Grease it with some of the remaining 10g butter (reserve the rest for greasing again).

Ladle the batter on to the hot pan in 75ml portions, leaving at least 5cm between each pancake. Flatten the pancakes slightly with the jug or ladle. Cook for 3–4 minutes per side, until the bases are golden and the edges are firm. Flip and continue cooking until golden, 3–4 minutes more. Transfer to the prepared baking sheet. The inside of the pancake will finish cooking in the oven. Make sure the pancake stay in the oven for about 5 minutes. Continue until you have used all the batter.

Heat the maple syrup and butter together in a small saucepan set over a medium heat, whisking to combine, 5–6 minutes. Serve the syrup with the pancakes.

RON WEASLEY'S BREAKUP CHICKEN NOODLE SOUP

✴

YIELD: 4 servings | PREP TIME: 15 minutes | COOK TIME: 20 minutes

---

As Ron recovers in the hospital from drinking poisoned mead that Professor Slughorn had inadvertently planned to give to Dumbledore, he is comforted by his close friend Hermione in *Harry Potter and the Half-Blood Prince*. Suddenly, Ron's girlfriend, Lavender Brown, bursts in, fretting about her 'Won-Won'.

Jessie Cave, who plays Lavender, appreciates her character's honesty about her emotions. When Lavender runs to Ron's bedside, 'She's furious she isn't already there and obviously worried and panic stricken about his state of health. Then she realizes Hermione's there, and she's just hurt.' Then Ron murmurs Hermione's name in his sleep. 'That crushes her,' says Cave. 'She realizes that's it. She's hurt, and she's heartbroken.'

This soup is inspired by a similar one Ron has at lunch while he tries to remember how exactly he broke up with Lavender. No matter which side of the breakup you are on, this brothy soup, featuring chicken breast, carrots, celery and egg noodles, is perfect for healing a broken heart.

- 15g unsalted butter
- 1 tablespoon olive oil
- 2 celery sticks, finely diced
- 2 carrots, peeled and finely diced
- 1 brown onion, finely diced
- 300g cooked chicken breast, diced
- 1 teaspoon salt
- ½ teaspoon pepper
- ½ teaspoon dried thyme
- ½ teaspoon dried oregano
- 1.4 litres vegetable stock
- 160g cooked egg noodles

In a large stockpot, heat the butter and olive oil over a medium heat until the butter is melted. Stir in the celery, carrots and onion and cook until softened, 7 to 8 minutes.

Add the chicken, salt, pepper, thyme, oregano and stock. Stir well. Bring to the boil and reduce the heat to low. Simmer for 10 minutes. Stir in the noodles. Taste and adjust seasonings as desired. Serve.

> **'TELL ME AGAIN HOW I BROKE UP WITH LAVENDER?'**
>
> – Ron Weasley, *Harry Potter and the Half-Blood Prince*

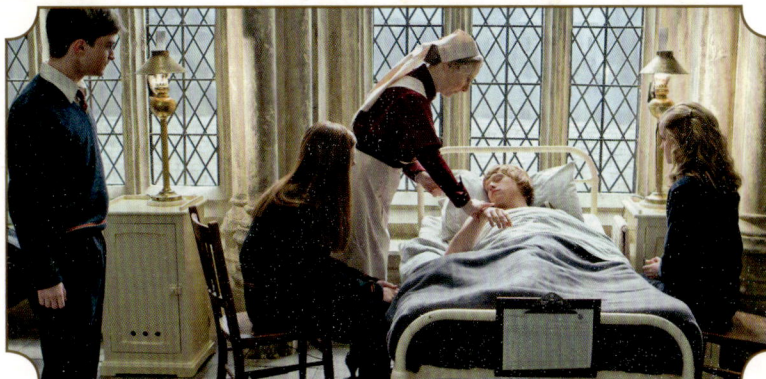

QUIDDITCH EGGS ON TOAST FOR THE WIN

GF* | YIELD: 4 servings | PREP TIME: 25 minutes | COOK TIME: 20 minutes

---

In *Harry Potter and the Half-Blood Prince*, Ron Weasley makes it on to the Gryffindor Quidditch team, but for his first game, the new Keeper seems more than a little nervous. Luckily, Ron has a good friend in Harry, who won a vial of Felix Felicis in Potions class. Luna believes she has seen him pour some of this 'Liquid Luck' into Ron's drink, which gives Ron all the confidence he needs to win the game.

Becoming the team's Keeper gave Rupert Grint a chance to play the game, which he had been looking forward to for years. 'Ron actually becomes a hero on the Quidditch team,' says Grint. 'He makes a few saves and starts feeling cocky. It's a side to Ron that you don't usually get to see.'

This fancy take on the poached egg on toast, as seen on the breakfast table in *Harry Potter and the Half-Blood Prince*, is a real keeper, featuring buttered toast topped with bacon rashers and a poached egg, assembled with a square centre and toast triangles all around.

- 8 slices bread
- 15g salted butter
- Splash of vinegar
- 4 medium eggs
- 4 rashers back bacon
- Salt
- Pepper
- 1 tablespoon chopped parsley (optional)

Toast the bread slices and lightly butter them on one side as they come out of the oven or toaster. Cut the edges off the toast, creating 8 squares. Using 4 of the slices, cut from corner to corner in an X, to create 4 triangles. Arrange 1 square piece of toast on each of 4 plates. Arrange the 4 triangles around the outside, on each edge. Continue until you have used all the bread.

Meanwhile, heat a pot of water about 10cm deep, add a splash of vinegar and bring to the boil over a high heat; then reduce the heat to low. Crack each egg one at a time into individual small bowls, then slide the eggs into the water one at a time, continuing until all eggs have been added. Be sure to add each egg far enough apart from the other eggs so that they do not touch. Cook for 4–7 minutes; when done, remove each egg with a slotted spoon.

While the eggs are cooking, fry the bacon in a large frying pan over a medium heat for 5–7 minutes, turning once, until cooked. Transfer each rasher a toast square. Top each with a poached egg. Season with salt and pepper to taste and parsley, if using, and serve immediately.

NOTE

This recipe is easily made gluten free by using gluten-free bread

'GOOD LUCK TODAY, RON.
I KNOW YOU'LL BE BRILLIANT.'

– Lavender Brown, *Harry Potter and the Half-Blood Prince*

GREAT HALL SWEET FRENCH TOAST WITH BERRY COMPOTE

★

V | Yield: 4 servings | PREP TIME: 15 minutes | COOK TIME: 45 minutes

It might be 1929 when the Scamander brothers, Jacob Kowalski and Lally Hicks join Dumbledore at Hogwarts in *Fantastic Beasts: The Secrets of Dumbledore*, but breakfast in the Great Hall seems very similar to what is served in the Harry Potter films. There are egg dishes, hog's-head-topped jugs and long metal racks of toast and other breads. Jacob enjoys a thick concoction of bread and butter as he shows off his 'wand' to second-year Gryffindors.

The scene in the Great Hall was filmed on a green-screen set, with the only practical parts being the tables and floor. 'We're not in these spaces for very long,' says visual effects supervisor Christian Manz, 'so it didn't make sense to build a massive set.'

Toast is a must at every Hogwarts breakfast, but this particular toast is magical. Brioche bread is dipped in a sweetened egg mixture with cinnamon and then pan-fried to perfection before it's topped with a sweetened berry compote, hitting all the right notes of sweetness and boldness.

BERRY COMPOTE
- 1 x 425–450g bag frozen mixed berries
- 50g caster sugar
- 1 tablespoon freshly grated ginger
- 1 teaspoon cinnamon
- 2 tablespoons lemon juice

FRENCH TOAST
- 3 medium eggs, beaten
- 60ml non-dairy milk such as almond or oat
- 1 teaspoon vanilla extract
- 1 teaspoon cinnamon
- 1 tablespoon soft light brown sugar
- Pinch salt
- 15g unsalted butter (or preferred non-dairy substitute)
- 1 loaf brioche bread, cut into 8 slices

TO MAKE THE BERRY COMPOTE:

In a large saucepan, combine the berries, sugar, ginger, cinnamon and lemon juice. Bring to the boil over a medium-high heat, then reduce the heat to medium-low heat. Cook for 4–5 minutes or until the berries begin to break down in the liquid that forms. Set aside until ready to serve.

TO MAKE THE FRENCH TOAST:

Preheat the oven to 110°C/90°C fan/Gas Mark ¼. Line a baking sheet with baking paper or foil and place in the oven.

In a wide-based mixing bowl, whisk together the eggs, non-dairy milk, vanilla, cinnamon, brown sugar and salt.

Heat a large frying pan over a medium heat. Melt a little of the butter – enough to lightly coat the pan – in the frying pan.

Working with one slice of bread at a time, coat on both sides with the egg mixture, then place in the frying pan. Do not crowd the slices and do not coat the bread until there is room to cook it. You will have to cook this French toast in batches. Cook until the bread is golden on both sides, flipping once, 4–5 minutes per side.

Transfer to the baking sheet in the oven.

Continue until all the bread has been cooked.

Drizzle the French toast with the berry compote and serve immediately.

PROFESSOR SPROUT'S VEGETABLE PATCH TART

V | YIELD: 4 servings | PREP TIME: 15 minutes | COOK TIME: 30 minutes

---

In Professor Sprout's second-year Herbology class, in *Harry Potter and the Chamber of Secrets*, the students' first lesson is how to repot Mandrakes. The pots of the squirming, squealing plant life completely cover the table that runs down Greenhouse Three, awaiting their transfer and replanting.

'The point of the scene is learning about the Mandrakes and putting them into new pots,' explains production designer Stuart Craig, 'so the focus and grouping of the set is staged around this massively long table covered with potted plants.' Other plants in the room include long vines with large, dark green leaves. One can only guess at the plants grown in Greenhouses One and Two.

Just as Professor Sprout's greenhouse is packed with plants, so is this dish. The puffed pastry tart is topped with asparagus and onions, and you can even eat it with your hands. A cool salad with lemon vinaigrette–dressed rocket and tomatoes provides a lovely contrast to the warm tart.

TART
1 sheet puff pastry, thawed

1 medium egg, beaten

225g asparagus, trimmed

2 slices red onion, halved

SALAD
80g baby rocket

1 medium tomato, sliced and quartered

2–4 tablespoons vinaigrette from the Slug Club Prawn and Chorizo Skewers (substitute thyme for chill flakes) (see page 65)

TO MAKE THE TART:

Preheat the oven to 200°C/180°C fan/Gas Mark 6. Line a baking sheet with baking paper and add the pastry on top. Brush it all over with egg.

Arrange the asparagus on the puff pastry (with stalks touching, if necessary), alternating which direction the top is facing. Fit the red onions around the asparagus. Place the baking sheet in the oven and bake for 25–30 minutes or until the puff pastry is puffed and golden.

TO MAKE THE SALAD:

In a large mixing bowl, toss together the rocket, tomato and vinaigrette. Heap it on to the puff pastry.

Cut into 4 equal rectangles and serve immediately.

> **'WELCOME TO GREENHOUSE THREE, SECOND YEARS. NOW, GATHER ROUND, EVERYONE.'**
> – Pomona Sprout, *Harry Potter and the Chamber of Secrets*

UNICORNS OF THE FORBIDDEN FOREST CHANGING VERMICELLI NOODLE CHICKEN SALAD

GF* | YIELD: 4 servings | PREP TIME: 20 minutes | COOK TIME: 10 minutes

Professor McGonagall gives Harry, Hermione, Ron and Draco a detention in *Harry Potter and the Philosopher's Stone*. As penance, they are escorted by Hagrid into the Forbidden Forest to look for injured unicorns. Harry and Draco find one of the magical creatures, with its white coat and spiralling horn, but they are too late to save it. On set, the unicorn in the Dark Forest was constructed with a fully articulated steel skeleton, although it was not required to move.

Based on a Vietnamese salad, this dish is full of veggies and chicken. But it is really special for its colour-changing noodles. The noodles are first dyed purple by the cabbage, but they change to pink when the vinaigrette is added. Look for bean thread noodles to use in this recipe because they take the colour best; rice vermicelli is easier to find, but the colour will be more subtle and the magic less impressive. Most essential is to add the vinaigrette last, when your guests are watching, because that's the most impressive part – as if by real magic.

- 250g red cabbage, sliced into ribbons
- 225g bean thread vermicelli noodles (aka glass noodles or cellophane noodles)
- 140g carrots, julienned
- 90g bean sprouts
- 140g cooked chicken, chopped
- 1 spring onion, thinly sliced
- 60ml seasoned rice vinegar
- 2 tablespoons soy sauce
- 2 tablespoons sesame oil
- 2 tablespoons clear honey
- 1 lime, cut into 8 wedges

In a medium saucepan, add the cabbage to 1 litre cold water. Set over a high heat and bring to the boil. Press down on the cabbage with the back of a wooden spoon. Reduce the heat to medium and continue boiling for 10 minutes.

Place the bean thread noodles in a large mixing bowl. Strain the cabbage water into the bowl with the noodles. Set the cabbage ribbons aside. Leave the noodles to sit for 10 minutes.

To a large bowl, add the carrots, bean sprouts, chicken and spring onion. Toss to mix well. Drain any remaining liquid from the noodles. Arrange the noodles, chicken mixture and cabbage ribbons in a serving bowl or on a platter.

In a small mixing bowl, whisk together the rice vinegar, soy sauce, sesame oil and honey.

When you add the vinaigrette to the noodle mixture, the noodles will change colour, so do this when you have an audience. Pour the vinaigrette over the noodles and then toss it all together. (Cue the oohs and ahhs!) Serve with lime wedges, for squeezing.

NOTE

This recipe is easily made gluten-free by using gluten-free soy sauce.

> 'YOU MEAN YOU-KNOW-WHO'S OUT THERE, RIGHT NOW, IN THE FOREST?'
> 'BUT HE'S WEAK. HE'S LIVING OFF THE UNICORNS.'
>
> – Hermione Granger and Harry Potter, *Harry Potter and the Philosopher's Stone*

YULE BALL SHERBET FIZZY

V, GF | YIELD: 4 servings | PREP TIME: 10 minutes

The Yule Ball, 'an evening of well-mannered frivolity', as described by Professor Minerva McGonagall, is the most anticipated social event of the year in *Harry Potter and the Goblet of Fire*. The celebration takes place over the Christmas holiday, giving the students a chance to dress up, attend a dance and possibly get or even cause a broken heart or two.

The Great Hall is entirely covered in silver decorations for the ball, but the Hogwarts house colours are represented in drinks dispensed from cauldron-shaped punch bowls. Rows of glasses filled with one of four pastel interpretations (pink for Gryffindor, green for Slytherin, gold for Hufflepuff and blue for Ravenclaw) curve around an ice-carved centrepiece.

This refreshing fizzy drink, inspired by the Yule Ball punch, is made with fizzy lemonade, grenadine and a scoop of sherbet. It is bright, sweet and a good choice to cool down with after an exhilarating party.

- 1 litre fizzy lemonade
- 2 tablespoons grenadine
- 200g lime or lime sorbet
- Gold lustre dust

Evenly divide the lemonade among four glasses. Add ½ tablespoon grenadine to each glass. Swirl gently. Drop in a scoop of sorbet (about 50g) and scatter with gold lustre dust. Serve.

'AT THE SECOND WAND STROKE, YOUR BEVERAGE WILL BE SERVED.'

– The Yule Ball Programme, *Harry Potter and the Goblet of Fire*

★ BEHIND THE MAGIC ★

Lines of long-necked bottles topped with clear-cast pumpkins and etched with a snowflake design separated the 'house drinks.'

PROFESSOR LUPIN'S FULL MOON SPRITZER

✦

V, V+, GF | YIELD: 4 servings | PREP TIME: 10 minutes

During the events of *Harry Potter and the Prisoner of Azkaban*, clues point to the deduction that Professor Remus Lupin is not just the favourite Defence Against the Dark Arts teacher. He also hides a tragic secret: he is a werewolf. When he teaches the Riddikulus Spell against Boggarts, the object he fears is a full moon. And not only does Severus Snape teach a lesson about these nocturnal beasts when he substitutes for Lupin's class, but he also stresses how to recognize a werewolf when assigning their homework.

David Thewlis, who plays Lupin, researched lycanthropy (werewolfism) because of his interest in the subject's history, but he uncovered more folklore than facts. 'There's nothing factually you can find out,' he says, 'so I thought there's no real point in playing Lupin overtly as a werewolf. There wouldn't be anything in his character that shows it.'

This refreshing spritzer, inspired by Professor Lupin's monthly transformations into a werewolf, has a delightful fruity, minty flavour that can be enjoyed under the bright orb of a full moon (or at any time of month).

2 teaspoons chopped mint, plus 4 whole mint leaves

150g blackberries

Ice (optional)

1 bottle cold pinot grigio

250ml soda water

2 tablespoons vanilla syrup

1 lime, cut into 8 wedges

SPECIALIST TOOLS
4 wine glasses, or double old fashioned glasses with a capacity of at least 350ml

To each glass, add ½ teaspoon chopped mint and 3 blackberries. Use the back of a spoon to muddle together the mint and the berries. Fill with ice, if using.

Skewer 2 blackberries and a whole mint leaf on cocktail sticks to garnish.

When you are ready to serve, pour in 175ml wine, 60ml soda water and ½ tablespoon vanilla syrup into each glass. Garnish with the blackberry cocktail sticks and 2 lime wedges. Top up with more wine, if desired.

'HE'S A WEREWOLF!'
– Hermione Granger, *Harry Potter and the Prisoner of Azkaban*

✦ BEHIND THE MAGIC ✦

Lupin has two scratches that run across his face visible in both his forms, to show the relationship between the man and beast.

WONDERWITCH PASSION JUICE SMOOTHIE

V, V+, GF | YIELD: 4 servings | PREP TIME: 10 minutes

WonderWitch is a line of products for young witches that's sold by Weasleys' Wizard Wheezes, featuring cosmetic items and love potions. Displayed in a tier of pink flower petals, the love potions are sold in heart-shaped bottles with names like Cupid Crystals and Flirting Fancies. 'They really do work,' guarantees co-owner George Weasley.

These potions do work – but it is important to have the right person drink it. In *Harry Potter and the Half-Blood Prince*, Harry returns to the Gryffindor common room to find that Ron has eaten a box of love-potion-laced chocolates from Romilda Vane, who has a crush on Harry. Ron becomes obsessed with Romilda, whom he has not even met, so Harry takes him to Potions Professor Horace Slughorn for an antidote.

This bold smoothie is sweet and tart, thanks to the combination of the acidic pineapple and sweet banana. Coconut water and bright strawberries balance out the flavours, for a lovely drink inspired by the pink of the WonderWitch products.

- 175g pineapple chunks
- 2 bananas, peeled
- 250ml coconut water
- 250g strawberries
- 2.5cm piece ginger
- 2 tablespoons dried dragon fruit (optional)

FOR GARNISHING
- 4 strawberries
- 4 pineapple chunks
- 4 cocktail sticks

Combine the pineapple, banana, coconut water, strawberries, ginger and dragon fruit, if using, in a blender and blend until smooth.

Divide among 4 glasses. Thread a strawberry and a pineapple chunk on to each of the 4 cocktail sticks. Rest a cocktail stick garnish on the edge of each glass. Serve.

> 'SEE THAT GIRL OVER THERE? THAT'S ROMILDA VANE. APPARENTLY SHE'S TRYING TO SMUGGLE YOU A LOVE POTION.'
>
> – Hermione Granger to Harry Potter, *Harry Potter and the Half-Blood Prince*

✷ BEHIND THE MAGIC ✷

Accompanying the box of chocolates is a card that reads, 'Dear Harry, Thinking sweet thoughts of you, Romilda,' as she blows him a kiss in a heart-shaped photo.

HAGRID'S PERFECT PUMPKIN SMOOTHIES

V, GF | YIELD: 4 servings | PREP TIME: 10 minutes

Pumpkins at Hogwarts are not just for the Halloween holiday, although they do add to the festivities by hovering about the students' heads in the Great Hall in *Harry Potter and the Philosopher's Stone*. But there is no worry about them falling down on to the tables – the digital pumpkins were assigned a horizon line by the visual artists that they could not drop beneath, much like the rain and snow that often fell there, too.

Hagrid grows pumpkins in a patch beside his hut in *Harry Potter and the Prisoner of Azkaban*. And because set decorator Stephenie McMillan always looked for opportunities to recycle or refresh props, the smaller pumpkins in the patch were used as moulds for the chocolate pumpkin-shaped cakes served at the dessert feast in *Harry Potter and the Goblet of Fire*.

This smoothie is a fun new take on one of the wizarding world's favourite drinks: Pumpkin Juice. The recipe combines apple juice, pumpkin purée, a banana and mixed spice for a perfectly refreshing smoothie.

- 500ml cold apple juice
- 250ml cold coconut water
- 225g pumpkin purée
- 1 frozen overripe banana
- 1 tablespoon clear honey
- 1 teaspoon mixed spice
- 4 cinnamon sticks, for garnish

Combine the apple juice, coconut water, pumpkin purée, banana, honey and mixed spice in a blender, and blend until smooth. Divide into 4 glasses. Garnish each glass with a cinnamon stick and serve immediately.

> 'WELL, WHAT DID YOU EXPECT – PUMPKIN JUICE?'
>
> – Madam Pomfrey, *Harry Potter and the Chamber of Secrets*

✦ BEHIND THE MAGIC ✦

When Seamus Finnigan wonders what Alastor Moody has in his flask in *Harry Potter and the Goblet of Fire*, Harry responds 'I don't know, but I don't think it's Pumpkin Juice.' He's right – it's Polyjuice Potion.

SORTING HAT SIPS

V, GF* | YIELD: 4 servings | PREP TIME: 20 minutes | COOK TIME: 5 minutes

---

The Sorting Hat places first-year Hogwarts students into one of four houses. Once the hat is placed on their head, it announces whether they are a Gryffindor, Hufflepuff, Ravenclaw or Slytherin.

The Sorting Hat started as a puppet, but as costume designer Judianna Makovsky recalls, 'It didn't look like a hat. It looked like a puppet.' So *Harry Potter and the Philosopher's Stone* director Chris Columbus asked her to make a Sorting Hat. 'I can make a hat,' she responded, 'but I can't make it talk.' When Makovsky showed her creation, 'Everyone said it was a beautiful hat,' she recalls. 'And then Robert Legato, the visual effects supervisor, asked, "Where does it talk?" And Chris said, "She made the hat. You make it talk!"'

These Sorting Hat Sips are shot glass-sized. Made with chocolate liqueur, a muddled raspberry and vodka, they are topped with a round sweet biscuit and a tear-shaped chocolate that perches on the rim of the glass, just like a hat.

- 50g dark chocolate
- 4 individually wrapped teardrop-shaped chocolates, unwrapped
- 4 small round sweet biscuits (about 5cm in diameter)
- 4 fresh raspberries
- 125ml chocolate liqueur
- 125ml raspberry vodka

Line a tray with greaseproof paper. Break the dark chocolate into pieces and place in a small microwave-safe bowl. Microwave for 30-second intervals, stirring after each one, until smooth. Dip the base of the teardrop chocolate into the melted chocolate and attach to the centre of the biscuit; repeat with all four. Once the teardrop chocolate is set on the biscuit, place the hat in the melted chocolate and use a spoon to cover the whole hat. Remove from the bowl by lifting out with a fork and tapping to allow the excess chocolate to be removed. Set on the prepared tray. Transfer the tray to the fridge and leave to cool completely to harden, about 30 minutes.

Place one raspberry in each of 4 shot glasses. Muddle the berries to break them apart. To each glass, add 30ml chocolate liqueur and 30ml raspberry vodka. Top with a biscuit hat. Serve.

'BETTER BE . . . GRYFFINDOR!'

– The Sorting Hat to Harry Potter,
Harry Potter and the Philosopher's Stone

★ **NOTE**

This recipe is easily made gluten-free by using gluten-free biscuits.

HOGSMEADE GINGER AND LIME BUTTERSCOTCH MUG

V, V+, GF | YIELD: 4 servings | PREP TIME: 5 minutes

During a trip to the wizarding village Hogsmeade, just outside Hogwarts, Harry catches the attention of Horace Slughorn at the popular watering hole The Three Broomsticks and receives an invitation to join him, along with Hermione and Ron (whom Slughorn calls Wallenby), for a drink.

Harry made a brief first visit to The Three Broomsticks in *Harry Potter and the Prisoner of Azkaban*. The pub's interior follows the same Tudor style as The Leaky Cauldron in London, with the added decoration of myriad stuffed deer heads on the walls. The Three Broomsticks set was created with rafters and trusses cast in plaster, to approximate old oak. Anything resembling timber was well-aged and distressed.

This drink creates a refreshing thirst-quencher by combining ginger ale, lime, bourbon and a 'Butterbeerish' butterscotch schnapps.

125ml bourbon

125ml butterscotch schnapps

1 x 350ml can ginger ale

1 lime, cut into 8 wedges

Into each of 4 ice-filled glasses, pour 30ml bourbon, 30ml butterscotch schnapps and 90ml ginger ale. Squeeze 1 lime wedge into each. Garnish each glass with a further lime wedge.

BEHIND THE MAGIC

A huge cask of Butterbeer is set behind the bar at The Three Broomsticks in *Harry Potter and the Prisoner of Azkaban.*

'THREE BUTTERBEERS AND SOME GINGER AND LIME, PLEASE.'

– Hermione Granger, *Harry Potter and the Half-Blood Prince*

RON'S LUCKY DAY SLURP

V, V+, GF | YIELD: 4 servings | PREP TIME: 5 minutes

Ron Weasley makes the Gryffindor Quidditch team in *Harry Potter and the Half-Blood Prince*, although not without the help of Hermione Granger, who uses a Confundus Charm against his strongest competition, Cormac McLaggen. Then Ron has to face his actual first game, and it is noticeable how nervous he is.

'Ron is really scared,' says Rupert Grint. 'You can see Ron was really hesitant in tryouts and not very balanced, even on a broom. In all honesty, he's not really good enough, I guess.'

'But Harry's won Felix Felicis, which is supposed to give you the confidence to do anything you want,' Grint continues. 'Harry pretends to slip it in his juice at breakfast. He doesn't really, but it gives Ron this feeling that he can do anything. And he actually does it on his own.' Gryffindor wins the game.

There is nothing confusing about this pomegranate–passion fruit drink, with or without the gin. It will bring good luck to your day to have a sip – or a slurp – of this refreshing drink with friends and family.

- 250ml passion fruit juice cocktail
- 250ml pomegranate juice
- 250ml tonic water
- 250ml gin (optional)
- 450g ice
- 4 maraschino cherries

Combine the passion fruit juice cocktail, pomegranate juice, tonic water, gin, if using, and ice in a jug and stir gently. Serve in 4 glasses, each with a maraschino cherry.

> 'YOU LOOK DREADFUL, RON.
> IS THAT WHY YOU PUT SOMETHING IN HIS CUP?'
>
> – Luna Lovegood, *Harry Potter and the Half-Blood Prince*

BEHIND THE MAGIC

As Rupert Grint and Freddie Stroma (Cormac) are roughly the same size, Stroma's shoulder guards were scaled up, and extra panels were added to the front and back of his uniform to make him appear bigger. Grint's uniform was constructed on the small side.

HOGWARTS HOT MULLED PUMPKIN CIDER

V, V+, GF | YIELD: 8 servings | PREP TIME: 5 minutes | COOK TIME: 15 minutes

The winter weather in the Scottish Highlands, where Hogwarts is located, can be very chilly. Hogsmeade, the only completely wizarding village in Great Britain, is permanently above the snow line, so keeping warm is a necessity.

Production designer Stuart Craig considered the Great Hall a communal place for the students and wanted a fireplace to be the centre of it all. Director Chris Columbus agreed. 'We built a lot of fire into the Great Hall,' he explains, 'for it needed to be this magical warm, loving place.' There may be another reason the ever-blazing fireplace was important to the set – Columbus remembers that when filming began on *Harry Potter and the Philosopher's Stone* at Leavesden Studios, the room was freezing cold.

For this recipe, cloudy apple juice is blended with pumpkin purée, mixed spice and cinnamon sticks, then heated before serving (but you could use apple cider instead of the juice if you prefer something stronger). On cold days, this warm version of a pumpkin-based drink will keep both Muggles and wizards toasty.

- 2 litres cloudy apple juice
- 225g pumpkin purée
- 1 tablespoon mixed spice
- 3 cinnamon sticks
- 2 tablespoons soft light brown sugar

Combine the apple juice, pumpkin purée, mixed spice, cinnamon sticks and brown sugar in a large pot. Stir well. Heat over a medium-high heat to boiling, stirring frequently. Cook for 10 minutes. Remove from the heat and leave to cool slightly before ladling into mugs, taking care not to ladle in any cinnamon sticks.

> 'WATCH YOURSELF ON THE STAIRS, IT'S A BIT ICY AT THE TOP.'
>
> – Cho Chang to Harry Potter, *Harry Potter and the Goblet of Fire*

✴ BEHIND THE MAGIC ✴

A hand-painted cyclorama with a view outside Hogwarts encircled the Great Hall set and changed with the seasons. When it was wintertime during the films, snow was painted on each of the mountaintops.

HALLOWEEN PUMPKIN CARROT SQUARES

V | YIELD: 12 servings | PREP TIME: 30 minutes | COOK TIME: 35 minutes, plus 2 hours cooling

---

The feast served at Harry Potter's first Halloween at Hogwarts, in *Harry Potter and the Philosopher's Stone*, concludes with an abundance of sweets. Tables are laden with cauldrons filled with lollipops, skull-shaped sugar confections and bowls of jelly drops. Many of these desserts reflect the bounty of the season: shiny apples, pumpkin juice and cakes topped with marzipan carrots. The Halloween feast is interrupted when Professor Quirinus Quirrell races into the room, shouting that a troll has entered the castle.

The foods served, especially the desserts, were always created with the thought of what would spoil or melt under the hot lights of the studio's soundstages. 'It's practicality that decides it, of course,' explains set decorator Stephenie McMillan.

With notes of both pumpkin cake and carrot cake, it is no trick that these squares are a year-round treat. The creamy icing and flaked almonds bring it all together.

PUMPKIN CARROT SQUARES

115g unsalted butter, softened, plus more for greasing

250g plain flour

2 teaspoons baking powder

1 teaspoon salt

2 teaspoons mixed spice (cinnamon can be substituted)

275g soft light brown sugar

2 medium eggs

225g pumpkin purée

1 teaspoon vanilla extract

110g carrots, freshly grated

ICING

115g unsalted butter, softened

225g cream cheese

45g marshmallow creme

125g icing sugar

1 teaspoon vanilla extract

Flaked almonds, for garnish

TO MAKE THE PUMPKIN CARROT SQUARES:

Preheat the oven to 180°C/160°C fan/Gas Mark 4. Grease the inside of a 33 x23cm baking dish.

In a large mixing bowl, sift together the flour, baking powder, salt and mixed spice. Set aside.

In the bowl of a stand mixer or a large mixing bowl if using a hand mixer, combine the brown sugar and butter, mixing on medium-low for 3 minutes. The mixture should be light and fluffy. Add the eggs, pumpkin purée and vanilla extract and mix on medium-low until combined. Add the carrots and mix briefly to incorporate.

With the mixer running on its lowest speed, add the flour mixture a little at a time until fully incorporated. Pour the batter into the prepared baking dish and tap gently to even out.

Bake for 28–32 minutes or until a skewer inserted into the centre of the cake comes out clean. Cool completely in the baking pan.

TO MAKE THE ICING:

Add the butter to the bowl of a stand mixer fitted with the paddle attachment or to a large mixing bowl if using a hand mixer. Beat for 2 minutes until fluffy. Add the cream cheese and beat for 1 minute until fully incorporated. Add the marshmallow creme, icing sugar and vanilla extract and beat for 2 minutes or until light and fluffy.

Spread the icing all over the pumpkin carrot cake. Garnish with flaked almonds. Cut into 12 squares. Enjoy immediately, or cover tightly and store at room temperature until you are ready to serve.

TRIWIZARD CHAMPIONS CAKE

V | YIELD: 1 cake | PREP TIME: 2 hours | COOK TIME: 2 hours

In *Harry Potter and the Goblet of Fire*, members from Beauxbatons Academy of Magic and Durmstrang Institute join Hogwarts students for the Triwizard Tournament – and are welcomed with a dessert feast that is a chocoholic's delight. 'We had feasts before,' said set decorator Stephenie McMillan, 'but we hadn't had a feast where we've seen this many desserts and puddings.'

The desserts were designed with three different colours of chocolate in mind, but director Mike Newell asked for other colours, to break up the brown of milk and dark chocolate. McMillan added jugs of a pink drink, along with some pink versions of the thousand white chocolate mice that wove through the other desserts on the tables.

As a tribute to the Triwizard Tournament and its three tasks, this three-layer cake of chocolate, banana and strawberry is topped with a vanilla and marshmallow creme icing. It's a mouthwatering welcome, whether to a Hogwarts event or at any other occasion.

STRAWBERRY LAYER
60ml rapeseed oil, plus more for greasing

125g plain flour

100g sugar

2 teaspoons baking powder

½ teaspoon coarse salt

1 medium egg

125ml milk

1 teaspoon strawberry extract

Red or pink food colouring, optional

TO MAKE THE STRAWBERRY LAYER:

Preheat the oven to 190°C/170°C fan/Gas Mark 5. Grease a 20cm round cake tin and fit the base with a piece of baking paper. Set aside.

In a medium mixing bowl, sift together the flour, sugar, baking powder and salt. Add the egg, milk, oil and strawberry extract and whisk vigorously for 2 minutes until smooth. If using, add the food colouring a few drops at a time and mix thoroughly until the desired colour is achieved.

Transfer the batter to the prepared cake tin and tap gently to even out. Bake for 15–20 minutes or until a skewer inserted into the centre comes out clean. Leave the oven on.

Loosen the cake around the edges of the tin by running a round-bladed knife around the perimeter. Remove from the tin and place the cake on a wire rack to cool completely.

TO MAKE THE BANANA LAYER:

Grease another 20cm cake tin (or clean the one used for the strawberry layer) and fit the base with a piece of baking paper. Set aside.

In a medium mixing bowl, sift together the flour, sugar, baking powder and salt. Add the egg, milk, oil and vanilla and whisk vigorously for 2 minutes until smooth. Stir in the mashed banana.

Continued on page 104

Continued from page 103

BANANA LAYER

60ml rapeseed oil, plus more for greasing

125g plain flour

100g sugar

2 teaspoons baking powder

½ teaspoon coarse salt

1 medium egg

125ml milk

1 teaspoon vanilla extract

1 ripe banana, mashed

CHOCOLATE LAYER

60ml rapeseed oil, plus more for greasing

125g plain flour

100g sugar

45g cocoa powder

2 teaspoons baking powder

½ teaspoon coarse salt

1 medium egg

125ml milk

1 teaspoon vanilla extract

125ml boiling water

ICING

675g unsalted butter, softened

1kg icing sugar

70g marshmallow creme

2 tablespoons vanilla extract

Sprinkles, sugar stars or other cake decorations, as desired

Transfer the batter to the prepared tin and tap lightly to even out. Bake for 15–20 minutes or until a skewer inserted into the centre comes out clean.

Loosen the cake around the edges of the tin by running a round-bladed knife around the perimeter. Remove from the tin and place the cake on a wire rack to cool completely.

TO MAKE THE CHOCOLATE LAYER:
Reduce the oven temperature to 180°C/160°C fan/Gas Mark 4. Grease another 23cm round cake tin (or clean the one used for the previous layers) and fit the base with a piece of baking paper. Set aside.

In a large mixing bowl, sift together the flour, sugar, cocoa powder, baking powder and salt with a whisk until evenly mixed.

Add the egg, milk, rapeseed oil and vanilla and whisk until smooth.

Pour the boiling water into the mixing bowl and whisk gently to combine. The batter will go from being really thick to being pourable and loose.

Transfer the batter to the prepared cake tin and tap gently to even out. Bake for 15–20 minutes or until a skewer inserted into the centre comes out clean.

Loosen the cake around the edges of the tin by running a round-bladed knife around the perimeter. Remove from the tin and place the cake on a wire rack to cool completely.

TO MAKE THE ICING:
Place the softened butter in the bowl of a stand mixer or a large mixing bowl if using a hand mixer. With the whisk attachment, beat until light and fluffy, 3–4 minutes. Add the icing sugar, marshmallow creme and vanilla extract. Beat again to incorporate.

TO ASSEMBLE THE CAKE:
Carefully slice the top dome off each cake.

Place the chocolate cake on a cake plate. Ice. Top with the banana cake. Ice. Top with the strawberry cake. Ice lightly all over to create a crumb coat. Chill for 20 minutes. Use the remaining icing to cover the cake and decorate as desired. A piping bag with a large star nozzle, or two, one opened and one closed, creates an easy border and topper. The icing can be dyed with food colouring for additional decoration.

'THIS CASTLE WILL NOT ONLY BE YOUR HOME THIS YEAR, BUT HOME TO SOME VERY SPECIAL GUESTS AS WELL.'

– Albus Dumbledore, *Harry Potter and the Goblet of Fire*

'THE MINISTRY IS WATCHING' PEAR GINGER PIE

V | YIELD: 1 pie | PREP TIME: 25 minutes | COOK TIME: 1 hour

During the opening feast for Harry's fifth year at Hogwarts, in *Harry Potter and the Order of the Phoenix*, the students are introduced to their new Defence Against the Dark Arts professor: Dolores Umbridge. Harry has already seen Umbridge at the Ministry of Magic, during his hearing for performing underage magic.

Imelda Staunton, who plays Umbridge, explains that the Ministry is afraid Dumbledore wants to take it over and change things. 'Well, the Ministry likes things how they are, to stay the same. So she has her eyes and ears open for any who are against the Ministry,' she says. 'That's what she believes in and she has to protect it.'

Umbridge's introduction comes at the end of the feast, and this recipe is inspired by one of the desserts served that night. Pear Ginger Pie has a distinct flavour, with a filling of D'Anjou pears and crystallized ginger. It is so good, the Ministry of Magic would close their eyes in happiness at the taste.

PASTRY

315g plain flour, plus more for work surface

1 teaspoon coarse salt

1 tablespoon icing sugar

1 teaspoon ground ginger

115g very cold unsalted butter

50g very cold solid vegetable fat

90ml ice water

2 tablespoons milk

TO MAKE THE PASTRY:

Preheat the oven to 190°C/170°C fan/Gas Mark 5. In a large bowl, combine the flour, salt, icing sugar and ginger. Cut the butter and vegetable fat into small pieces. Using a pastry cutter or two forks, work the butter and fat into the flour mixture until all the pieces are pea size or smaller.

Add the ice water a little at a time and use the pastry cutter to bring the dough together. As the dough comes together, switch to your hands or a spatula, adding more water until the dough just comes together. On a lightly floured surface, roll out half the dough and fit it into a deep 23cm pie dish. Roll out the second half of the dough and transfer it to a baking sheet. Refrigerate both while preparing the filling.

FILLING

- 1.4kg (about 6) D'Anjou pears, peeled, cored and diced
- 50g caster sugar
- 55g soft light brown sugar
- 20g crystallized ginger, chopped
- 30g cornflour
- 2 tablespoons lemon juice
- 1 tablespoon grated ginger
- 1 teaspoon cinnamon

TO MAKE THE FILLING:

In a large bowl, toss together the pears, caster sugar, brown sugar, crystallized ginger, cornflour, lemon juice, grated ginger and cinnamon.

When the filling is ready, set the pie dish on a rimmed baking sheet and fill with the pear mixture.

Top with the second pastry. Crimp the edges to seal. Cut 4 long slits and 4 short slits, alternating in a pattern around the top. Brush with the milk.

Place the pie in the oven and bake for 45–55 minutes or until golden. Remove from the oven and leave to cool for 1 hour before serving.

> 'AND HOW LOVELY TO SEE YOUR BRIGHT, HAPPY FACES SMILING UP AT ME.'
>
> – Dolores Umbridge, *Harry Potter and the Order of the Phoenix*

✴ NOTE

If you wish, you can give this pie a lattice top, to be more in line with a classic Pear Ginger Pie. To do so, cut the second round of pastry into 1cm-wide strips using a pizza wheel. On a baking paper-lined baking sheet, lay about half of the strips across, leaving 1cm between them. Pull back every other strip halfway and place one strip perpendicularly to the others. Return the 3 strips so they extend across the pie and pull back the other 3 strips in the same direction. Place another strip of pastry across the piece perpendicularly, leaving 1cm between it and the one next to it. Continue until half of the pie has been covered in lattice. Repeat on the other half. Chill with the pastry case. Fill the pastry case, gently flip the chilled lattice on top of the filling, peel away the paper and press the pastry strips into the case to seal the edges. Bake as instructed.

CRABBE AND GOYLE'S SLEEPY VANILLA BEAN RASPBERRY TARTLETS

✦

V | YIELD: 6 servings | PREP TIME: 20 minutes | COOK TIME: 4+ hours

To locate the Heir of Slytherin in *Harry Potter and the Chamber of Secrets*, Hermione devises a plan: disguise themselves as Slytherin students by taking Polyjuice Potion and then infiltrate the Slytherin common room. Their targets: Draco Malfoy's 'henchmen', Crabbe and Goyle, for whom Hermione bakes a sleeping potion into a pair of tiny, tantalizing cakes. (Hermione mistakenly uses a hair from Millicent Bulstrode's cat in her own potion and cannot go.)

Once transformed, the actors who play Crabbe and Goyle impersonate Harry and Ron. 'It was very tricky, but we had a lot of rehearsals,' says Josh Herdman (Goyle). The actors were asked to perform the scene in front of the producers before filming. 'So we watched the first film about ten times, studying Dan's and Rupert's mannerisms.'

These small tartlets, with a cheesecake filling and topped with fresh raspberries and a drizzle of raspberry jam, will awaken your taste buds with their big taste.

BASE
125g digestive or ginger biscuit crumbs

1 tablespoon sugar

45g salted butter, melted

FILLING
350g cream cheese

150g caster sugar

1½ tablespoons soured cream

1½ tablespoons fresh lime juice

175ml double cream

18 fresh raspberries

3 tablespoons raspberry jam

SPECIALIST TOOLS
Jumbo, 6-hole muffin tin

Jumbo muffin cases

TO MAKE THE BASE:
Line each hole in the tin with a muffin case. In a medium bowl, mix together the biscuit crumbs, sugar and melted butter until thoroughly combined. Divide the mixture equally among the bases of the 6 muffin cases, and press down and up the sides a bit with the back of a spoon or your fingers. Refrigerate while you make the filling.

TO MAKE THE FILLING:
In a medium bowl using a hand mixer, or in the bowl of a stand mixer fitted with a paddle attachment, cream together the cream cheese, sugar, soured cream and lime juice on medium speed until light and fluffy, about 3 minutes. Set aside. In another medium bowl, whip the double cream on high speed until stiff peaks form; then fold it into the cream cheese mixture. Remove the bases from the refrigerator and spoon filling into each one. Refrigerate for at least 4 hours – or, even better, overnight.

When ready to serve, top each with 3 raspberries. In a small microwave-safe bowl, microwave the raspberry jam for 20 seconds or until it moves easily. Drizzle over the tartlets. Serve.

'I FILLED THESE WITH A SIMPLE SLEEPING DRAUGHT. SIMPLE, BUT POWERFUL.'

– Hermione Granger, *Harry Potter and the Chamber of Secrets*

TRIWIZARD TOURNAMENT CHOCOLATE ROULADE

✳

V | YIELD: 1 cake | PREP TIME: 1 hour | COOK TIME: 45 minutes

---

After serving roasts, hams and chicken drumsticks in the Great Hall dinners throughout the Harry Potter films, set decorator Stephenie McMillan wanted a different look for a noteworthy feast. This particular celebration thus became a feast of desserts to welcome the students from the Beauxbatons and Durmstrang schools to the Triwizard Tournament in *Harry Potter and the Goblet of Fire*.

Chocolate frogs sit atop shiny iced cakes, and phoenix-adorned cakes rest on the headmaster's table for Dumbledore and his counterparts. There are profiterole 'explosions' and towers of No-Melt ice cream, along with giant wobbling chocolate trifles and jelly custards.

This dessert, based on one served to the students' tables, has three distinct flavour profiles in one cake, reflecting the Triwizard Tournament and its three tasks. A chocolate roulade is a rolled cake with cream inside. This one is drizzled with chocolate ganache, dusted with icing sugar and then topped with fresh strawberries for a winning combination.

CAKE

- 175g dark chocolate
- 2 tablespoons milk
- 6 eggs
- 95g icing sugar, plus more for dusting
- 30g unbleached plain flour
- 1 tablespoon cocoa powder

TO MAKE THE CAKE:

Preheat the oven to 190°C/170°C fan/Gas Mark 5. Line a 33 x23cm Swiss roll tin with baking paper.

On the hob over a medium heat, combine the chocolate and milk in a small saucepan, stirring until melted. Remove from heat and set aside.

Combine the eggs and icing sugar in a large mixing bowl and beat with a wire whisk until the mixture is pale and foamy, about 10 minutes. Beat in the chocolate mixture a little at a time until well combined. Sift together the flour and cocoa in a small mixing bowl and then add it to the egg mixture, folding to combine.

Pour the batter into the prepared tin and smooth out. Place into the oven and cook for 7–10 minutes. Remove the tin from the oven and turn out the cake on to a fresh sheet of baking paper dusted with icing sugar. Peel away the old paper. Roll the cake into a log shape, allowing the paper to roll with the cake, and place the roll on a wire rack to cool completely.

TO MAKE THE FILLING:

Continued on page 112

✳ BEHIND THE MAGIC ✳

Among set decorator Stephenie McMillan's favourite puddings was a ribbon cake that she imagined was filled with 'a most delicious heavy, chocolaty filling made with rum inside.'

Continued from page 110

FILLING

300ml double cream

2 tablespoons icing sugar

1 tablespoon cornflour

10 large strawberries, hulled and sliced

TOPPING

55g white chocolate

Icing sugar, for dusting

4 large strawberries, hulled and halved

In a large mixing bowl, use a handheld mixer to combine the double cream, icing sugar and cornflour. Mix on medium speed until the whipped cream mixture holds stiff peaks, 3–4 minutes.

Unroll the cooled cake, allowing it to rest on the paper it was rolled with. Cut a thin strip from each of the sides to remove the edges. Cover the roulade evenly with the whipped cream filling, then spread the sliced strawberries on top. Roll the cake back up, removing the paper as you roll the cake into a log. Transfer to a serving dish.

TO MAKE THE TOPPING:

Break the white chocolate into pieces and add to a microwave-safe bowl. Microwave on high for 20 seconds, stir and microwave again for 20 seconds (if needed). The white chocolate is done when it is melted into a smooth liquid. Sift icing sugar all over the cake. Drizzle with half of the white chocolate. Arrange the strawberries on top, pressing them into the chocolate. Either hold the berries in place for a minute or two, to allow the white chocolate secure them, or use cocktail sticks to temporarily keep them on top. Drizzle with the remaining white chocolate. Chill in the refrigerator for at least 15 minutes before serving.

> **'AS FROM THIS MOMENT, THE TRIWIZARD TOURNAMENT HAS BEGUN.'**
>
> – Albus Dumbledore, *Harry Potter and the Goblet of Fire*

HAGRID'S PUMPKIN PUDDING

✦

V, GF | YIELD: 6 servings | PREP TIME: 5 minutes | COOK TIME: 20 minutes

---

Puddings are synonymous with desserts and these, of course, include boiled and steamed puddings, as seen on the tables during the Halloween feast in *Harry Potter and the Philosopher's Stone*. Through ten years of filming Harry Potter films, the props and set design crew learned much about what real food could be served at meals in the Great Hall and what needed to be replicated in inedible forms.

'What tended to happen after the second film,' says prop modeller Pierre Bohanna, 'is that whenever the feast was shown, you got it at the end, so we did do a lot more puddings and other desserts.' Set decorator Stephenie McMillan also wanted these dishes to please the children, and with the wide variety of sweets, 'it was fun to push things to extremes.'

It is possible that Hagrid, who has a thriving pumpkin patch next to his hut, supplied veggies for Hogwarts feasts, which inspired this sweet pumpkin–flavoured pudding.

- 100g soft light brown sugar
- 2 tablespoons cornflour
- 350ml milk
- 225g pumpkin purée
- 1 teaspoon mixed spice
- 1 teaspoon vanilla extract

In a medium saucepan, stir together the brown sugar, cornflour, milk and pumpkin purée. Turn the heat to medium and cook, stirring constantly, until boiling. Reduce the heat to low and stir in the mixed spice. Continue cooking for about 2 minutes until thickened. Remove from the heat and stir in the vanilla extract.

Divide the pudding evenly among 6 bowls. Place in the refrigerator and chill completely before serving.

> **'I HOPE THERE'S PUDDING.'**
>
> – Luna Lovegood, *Harry Potter and the Order of the Phoenix*

✦ BEHIND THE MAGIC ✦

Puddings come in an assortment of forms: The dessert that Dobby drops on Mrs Mason's head in *Harry Potter and the Chamber of Secrets* is known as a Windtorte Pudding.

WEASLEY AND WEASLEY INSPIRED FUDGE

✳

V, GF | YIELD: 16 servings | PREP TIME: 5 minutes | COOK TIME: 20 minutes

---

Entrepreneurs Fred and George Weasley, who successfully sold their Skiving Snackboxes in *Harry Potter and the Order of the Phoenix*, open Weasleys' Wizard Wheezes in *Harry Potter and the Half-Blood Prince*. Their shop features the best-selling boxes and their individual items: Nosebleed Nougats, Fainting Fancies, Puking Pastilles and Fever Fudge.

Half of these sweets is charmed to create physical ailments to get a student out of class (known as 'skiving'); the other half serves as an antidote. Prop makers used more than 280 litres of silicone to manufacture the shockingly coloured treats for the shop displays. Barrels and cauldrons held thousands of these sweets.

This peanut butter and chocolate fudge is inspired by one sweet in the Weasley twins' Skiving Snackbox. The original Fever Fudge would get a student out of class with a fake malaise, but if the sweet treats in this book raise your temperature, it is only because your enjoyment of them reaches a fever pitch.

PEANUT BUTTER LAYER
Butter or oil, for greasing

200g caster sugar

60ml milk

125g smooth peanut butter

½ teaspoon vanilla extract

Pinch salt

CHOCOLATE LAYER
225g dark chocolate chips

300g sweetened condensed milk

½ teaspoon vanilla extract

TO MAKE THE PEANUT BUTTER LAYER:
Grease 20cm-square cake tin.

In a medium saucepan, combine the sugar and milk. Bring to the boil over a medium heat, stirring constantly. Boil for 2 minutes. Remove from heat and add the peanut butter, vanilla and salt. Stir until smooth.

Pour the mixture into the prepared cake tin and smooth gently. Tap the pan, if needed, to even it out. Set aside.

TO MAKE THE CHOCOLATE LAYER:
In a medium saucepan, combine the chocolate chips and condensed milk. Stir over a medium heat until smooth, 8–10 minutes. Remove from the heat and stir in the vanilla extract.

Pour the mixture over the peanut butter layer and spread evenly.

Chill in the refrigerator for 1 hour.

Cut into sixteen 2.5cm squares and serve. Leftovers should be stored in an airtight container and eaten within a week.

✳ **BEHIND THE MAGIC** ✳

Says James Phelps (Fred Weasley), 'The set for Weasleys' Wizard Wheezes had so much in it that you could stay in there for days and not see it all.'

'SKIVING SNACKBOXES: SWEETS THAT MAKE YOU ILL. GET OUT OF CLASS WHENEVER YOU LIKE. OBTAIN HOURS OF PLEASURE FROM UNPROFITABLE BOREDOM. CARE FOR ANOTHER?'

– Fred and George Weasley, *Harry Potter and the Order of the Phoenix*

HALF-BLOOD PRINCE COCONUT TARTLETS

V | YIELD: 12 mini pies | PREP TIME: 30 minutes | COOK TIME: 30 minutes

Harry is late for the opening feast in *Harry Potter and the Half-Blood Prince* due to a fight with Draco Malfoy on the Hogwarts Express. When he does arrive, it is with a recently broken nose, repaired courtesy of Luna Lovegood, who healed it with the Episkey spell.

Harry's broken nose was a collaboration between make-up designer Amanda Knight and special make-up designer Nick Dudman because it included small prosthetics. The final faux nose went through several iterations. 'It had to be nasty but comedic,' says Dudman. 'It took a while to come up with a shape people could look at and go, yes, that's horrible, but it's funny, too.'

As Hermione waits impatiently for Harry to arrive, others, including Ginny and Ron – especially Ron – are finishing off the dessert course of the feast. This recipe was inspired by a platter of small pastries and a creamy topping. These particular single-serving coconut cream tartlets are totally worth waiting for.

PASTRY
300g plain flour, plus more for dusting

1 teaspoon coarse salt

1 tablespoon icing sugar

115g very cold unsalted butter, cut into small pieces

50g very cold solid vegetable fat, cut into small pieces

90ml ice water

Egg wash (1 egg whisked with 1 tablespoon water)

FILLING
70g desiccated coconut

100g sugar

2 tablespoons cornflour

1 x 400g can full-fat coconut milk

1 teaspoon vanilla extract

TO MAKE THE PASTRY:

In a large bowl, combine the flour, salt and icing sugar. Using a pastry cutter or two forks, work the butter and shortening into the flour mixture until all the pieces are pea-sized or smaller.

Add the ice water a little at a time and use the pastry cutter to bring the dough together. Switch to your hands or a spatula, adding more water until the dough just comes together. On a lightly floured surface, roll out half the dough.

Use a 7.5cm round biscuit cutter to cut circles in the dough. Then fit each circle into the hole of a muffin tin. Continue until 16 circles have been cut and placed (you may need to make two batches or use two tins). Chill for 15 minutes and preheat the oven to 200°C/180°C fan/Gas Mark 6.

Prick the base of each pastry with a fork and brush with the egg wash. Bake for 12–15 minutes or until lightly browned. Cool completely.

TO MAKE THE FILLING:

In a dry frying pan set over a medium heat, toast the coconut, stirring constantly, until golden, 2–3 minutes. Transfer to a small bowl.

In a medium saucepan, stir together the sugar, cornflour and coconut milk. Turn the heat to medium and cook, stirring constantly, until boiling. Reduce the heat to low and continue cooking for 2–3 minutes until thickened (the pudding should coat the spoon). Remove from heat and stir in the vanilla extract. Stir in 35g of the toasted coconut.

Divide the pudding evenly among the prepared pastry cases. Top with the remaining toasted coconut. Chill in the refrigerator for 30 minutes before serving.

WIZARD CHESS CHESSBOARD BISCUITS

V | YIELD: about 18 biscuits | PREP TIME: 1 hour | COOK TIME: 15 minutes

---

The titular object of *Harry Potter and the Philosopher's Stone* produces the Elixir of Life, which bestows immortality. When the stone is stored at Hogwarts, it is protected by tests of skill that the professors hope will thwart Voldemort from acquiring it.

The final test is a life-sized game of wizard chess, where Ron has the chance to shine. The marble squares of the room-sized chessboard were created using a well-known faux-marbleization technique. Oil paint was squirted into a vat of water – in this case, a half-metre-square tank – and then paper was placed on top to absorb the swirl of colours. 'Once the paper is removed and dried,' explains production designer Stuart Craig, 'the best parts are digitally photographed, then reproduced on printers that can create stronger sheets up to 12 feet [3.6 metres] wide.'

For this recipe, the winning combination of chocolate and vanilla sugar biscuits creates a pattern that's reminiscent of chessboard squares.

225g salted butter, softened

200g granulated sugar

1 egg, plus 1 egg yolk

1 teaspoon vanilla

375g plain flour

1½ teaspoons baking powder

½ teaspoon coarse salt

30g black cocoa powder

Cream the butter and sugar together in the bowl of a stand mixer for 2 minutes or until even and light.

Add in the egg, yolk and vanilla and mix until smooth. In a medium bowl, combine the flour, baking powder and salt.

Add the flour mixture to the butter mixture slowly, mixing until just combined.

Split the dough in two, removing one half from the bowl. Add the black cocoa powder to the remaining dough and mix until evenly combined.

Roll each dough into a log about 15cm long and press down on each side to turn the circular log into a rectangular shape with square sides. Make sure both square logs are the same size and shape. Wrap dough in clingfilm and refrigerate for 1 hour.

Remove each dough log and cut each log into 3 equal-shaped strips lengthways. Rotate the logs and cut into thirds again, resulting in 9 equal-sized strips.

Continued on page 118

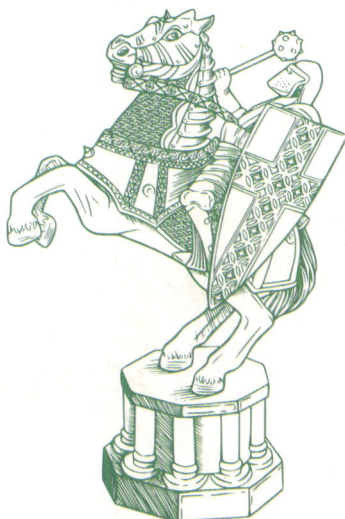

Continued from page 117

★ **BEHIND THE MAGIC** ★

To Rupert Grint, filming the wizard chess scene was 'so cool! The set was huge, and it was incredible when the pieces got smashed.' Grint still has a broken piece of the horse he rode as a knight.

Now it's time to make the 'chessboard'. Lay one vanilla strip, then one chocolate strip, then another vanilla strip next to each other. Top these strips with the alternating colours (chocolate, vanilla, chocolate), and then top once again with the same colours as the first row. Press the dough together to make a tight square, then wrap in clingfilm and refrigerate for another 30 minutes.

Repeat with the other set of dough.

While the dough chills, preheat the oven to 180°C/160°C fan/Gas Mark 4 and line a large baking sheet with baking paper.

Slice the chilled dough log into 5mm-thick biscuits and place on the baking sheet.

Bake for 9–10 minutes or until firm and just beginning to brown. Cool on a wire rack.

'YOU DON'T SUPPOSE THIS IS GOING TO BE LIKE REAL WIZARD CHESS?'
'YES, HERMIONE. I THINK THIS IS GOING TO BE EXACTLY LIKE WIZARD CHESS.'

– Hermione Granger and Ron Weasley, *Harry Potter and the Philosopher's Stone*

GET WELL
HALF MOON BISCUITS

✦

V | YIELD: about 40 biscuits | PREP TIME: 2 hours 20 minutes | COOK TIME: 45 minutes

---

Harry Potter prevents Quirinus Quirrell – and, therefore Voldemort, who had been sharing his body – from acquiring the Philosopher's Stone during their fatal encounter at the climax of *Harry Potter and the Philosopher's Stone*. Harry wakes up afterwards in the hospital wing, scratched and bruised, but delighted when he sees a large array of packaged confections at the foot of his bed.

Harry was able to keep the stone from Voldemort's hands, as Dumbledore tells him, for only those who wanted to find it but not use it would be able to get it. The Philosopher's Stone was cast by the prop makers, but at first it looked just like a ruby-coloured piece of boiled sweet. This challenge was solved by placing a flame above the camera, which gave it the shimmering appearance of a real gem.

Among the many gifts bestowed on Harry after his success is a clingfilm-wrapped bag of half moon-shaped biscuits. These vanilla crescents guarantee a good feeling all around.

BISCUITS

185g icing sugar

225g unsalted butter, softened

2 teaspoons vanilla extract

1 medium egg

325g plain flour, plus more for dusting

2 teaspoons baking powder

✦ **BEHIND THE MAGIC** ✦

During the early Harry Potter films, Daniel Radcliffe and Rupert Grint competed to see who had the biggest cut or bruise applied by the make-up team – a good idea until they realized how much time they had to spend in the make-up chair.

TO MAKE THE BISCUITS:

In the bowl of a stand mixer fitted with the paddle attachment or a large mixing bowl if using a hand mixer, combine the icing sugar, butter, vanilla extract and egg. Beat together the ingredients on the lowest speed until smooth. Add the flour and baking powder and mix again on low to combine. Scrape down the sides of the bowl and mix briefly once more.

Cover the bowl with clingfilm and chill in the refrigerator for 2 hours.

Preheat the oven to 190°C/170°C fan/Gas Mark 5. Line a baking sheet with baking paper.

Lightly flour a work surface. Roll out a little bit of dough at a time (keeping the remaining dough chilled) with a rolling pin (adding more flour as needed to avoid sticking) to 5mm thick. Use a 7.5cm round biscuit cutter to cut circles and then offset the biscuit cutter to create half moon-shaped biscuits. Either use the remaining diamond shape to decorate or re-roll into circles again. Continue, rolling out more dough as needed, until all the dough has been used. Place the half moons on the prepared baking sheet and bake for 7–8 minutes or until the very edge of the base is golden.

Remove from the oven and transfer the biscuits to a wire cooling rack. Cool completely.

Continued on page 122

Continued from page 121

ICING

- 500g icing sugar
- 3 tablespoons meringue powder or 2½ egg whites
- 90ml lukewarm water
- Gel food colouring, blue, purple and/or silver (optional)
- Gold lustre dust, sugar and edible foil stars (optional)

TO MAKE THE ICING:

In a large mixing bowl, combine the icing sugar, meringue powder or egg whites and water. Beat with a hand mixer on medium speed (or use a stand mixer with the whisk attachment) for 5–7 minutes. The icing is done when it's smooth, glossy and holds stiff peaks.

To colour the icing, add the desired amount of gel food colouring and stir until uniformly coloured. To make multiple colours, transfer the icing to separate bowls before colouring.

Spoon the icing into a piping bag fitted with a small, round nozzle. Pipe on to the biscuits as desired. To create the swirled effect, pipe a border on to each biscuit with stiff icing in one colour. Dilute the other colours with a little water until they are the consistency of a thick batter (this is called flooding icing). Spoon the flooding icing in different colours on to the biscuits and swirl together with a wooden skewer. If using, scatter the sanding sugar or stars on now. Leave the biscuits on the wire rack to harden. If desired, once the biscuits are dry, they can be brushed with lustre dust.

Biscuits should be stored in an airtight container at room temperature for up to a week.

> **'AH. TOKENS FROM YOUR ADMIRERS.'**
>
> – Albus Dumbledore, *Harry Potter and the Philosopher's Stone*

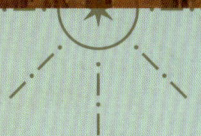

Chapter Three

GREAT HALL FEASTS

START-OF-TERM DRUMSTICKS WITH FLUFFY FEAST ROLLS AND CORN WITH GARLIC AND PARMESAN

YIELD: 8 servings | PREP TIME: 20 minutes | COOK TIME: 1 hour

The house-elves were only fictional heroes: the props department did the actual 'catering' for the feasts in the Great Hall throughout the Harry Potter films. For *Harry Potter and the Philosopher's Stone*, the designers needed to decide whether to use real food or replicas for a week-long shoot of the first Great Hall feast, featuring whole turkeys, chicken drumsticks, ears of corn and mashed potatoes. Director Chris Columbus wanted to use real food, but the dishes needed to be changed continually to keep the food from spoiling under the lights. Four mobile kitchens were placed around the set to accommodate this.

These chicken drumsticks, seasoned with a dry rub and served with baguettes, are inspired by the platters of drumsticks shown at the Hogwarts start-of-term feast in *Harry Potter and the Philosopher's Stone*. They are accompanied by a corn dish featuring garlic, herbs and Parmesan cheese.

DRUMSTICKS

Butter or oil, for greasing

55g cornflakes cereal

1 teaspoon dried rosemary

1 teaspoon dried sage

1 teaspoon dried thyme

1 teaspoon salt

½ teaspoon pepper

55g unsalted butter

2 tablespoons milk

8 chicken drumsticks
(about 1kg in total)

TO MAKE THE DRUMSTICKS:

Preheat the oven to 220°C/200°C fan/Gas Mark 7. Grease an oven-safe 33 x 23cm dish.

Place the cereal in a resealable bag and crush with a rolling pin. Add the rosemary, sage, thyme, salt and pepper to the bag and shake to incorporate. Set aside.

Melt the butter in a small frying pan over a medium heat. Remove from the heat and leave to cool for a few minutes. Whisk in the milk. Roll each chicken piece in the butter mixture, transfer it to the resealable bag and shake until it is coated all over. Place the chicken in the prepared dish, keeping the pieces separate and not touching.

Place the dish in the oven and bake for 40–50 minutes until the chicken is cooked through.

BAGUETTES

8 baguettes

30g salted butter, cut into 8 pieces

CORN

2 tablespoons olive oil

3 cloves garlic, very finely chopped

300g frozen corn, steamed

½ teaspoon coarse salt

¼ teaspoon pepper

25g Parmesan cheese, freshly grated

2 tablespoons diced roasted red peppers

✳ BEHIND THE MAGIC ✳

Instead of using cooked food for *Harry Potter and the Chamber of Secrets*, samples of real food were frozen so that moulds could be made of them and copies could then be cast in resin.

TO PREPARE THE BAGUETTES:

During the last 15 minutes of cooking the chicken, cut a slit into each baguette and slide in a piece of butter. Place the baguettes in the oven with the chicken for 8–10 minutes until they are warmed through.

TO MAKE THE CORN:

In a small frying pan, heat the olive oil over a medium heat. Add the garlic and cook, stirring, until fragrant, about 2 minutes. In a medium mixing bowl, combine the corn, garlic oil, salt, pepper, Parmesan and roasted red peppers. Toss well to combine. Serve immediately.

> **'LET THE FEAST BEGIN.'**
>
> – Albus Dumbledore, *Harry Potter and the Philosopher's Stone*

HOGWARTS ROAST CHICKEN WITH MARVELLOUS HASSELBACK ROASTED POTATOES AND GREEN BEAN SALAD

★

GF | YIELD: 6 servings | PREP TIME: 20 minutes | COOK TIME: 1 hour

The Great Hall at Hogwarts is a multipurpose room that hosts start-of-term feasts, duelling club competitions and even a ball in the Harry Potter films. The Great Hall was inspired by a sixteenth-century hall in one of the most famous Oxford colleges, Christ Church, and also by Westminster Hall in the Houses of Parliament. Production designer Stuart Craig realized that this place of meals and celebrations needed the durability of its influences, so the design team laid down a real stone floor. This lasted through ten years of filming the on-screen Hogwarts students and professors walking, running and dancing on it.

Four 30-metre tables and eight 30-metre benches were created for the room. 'Making was the obvious choice in this case,' says set decorator Stephenie McMillan, 'because there's nowhere I know where you could buy or rent them.'

A recipe fit for any Hogwarts event, this whole roasted chicken seasoned with a dry rub is served with Hasselback potatoes (roasted potatoes that are partially sliced so they fan out when cooked) and accompanied by a warm green bean salad with fried onions and ham.

CHICKEN

2.25–2.5kg whole chicken

30g cold unsalted butter, cut into 5mm-thick slices

1 teaspoon garlic powder

1 teaspoon paprika

1 teaspoon dried rosemary

1 teaspoon coarse salt

TO MAKE THE CHICKEN:

Preheat the oven to 230°C/210°C fan/Gas Mark 8. Line a baking sheet with foil and set a wire rack on top.

Place the chicken on the rack. Be sure to remove any giblets from inside the chicken. Slide the slices of butter under the chicken skin, arranging them around the chicken breast and legs.

In a small bowl, mix the garlic powder, paprika, rosemary and salt. Season all over the chicken, taking care to get it in as many places as possible. Place the chicken in the oven and roast for 20 minutes.

TO MAKE THE POTATOES:

Clean each potato and cut slices about 5mm apart into the potatoes (leaving the base 1cm uncut). In a small bowl, mix the olive oil, garlic powder, paprika, salt and rosemary.

Continued on page 135

MAINS

132

Continued from page 132

POTATOES

4 medium Maris Piper
   potatoes

2 tablespoons olive oil

1 teaspoon garlic powder

1 teaspoon paprika

1 teaspoon coarse salt

1 teaspoon dried rosemary

GREEN BEAN SALAD

350g fresh green beans,
   topped and tailed

1½ teaspoons olive oil

1 small onion, diced

2 tablespoons cider vinegar

1½ teaspoons soft light
   brown sugar

½ teaspoon coarse salt

¼ teaspoon pepper

75g ham, diced

Reduce the oven heat to 190°C/170°C fan/Gas Mark 5. Remove the baking sheet from the oven and place the potatoes on the baking sheet with the chicken. Brush the potatoes with half of the seasoning and oil mixture. Return the baking sheet to the oven and continue roasting for 1–1¼ hours, removing once about 10 minutes before the time is up to brush the potatoes with the remaining oil mixture. The chicken is done when an internal temperature reaches 74°C, or if you do not have a meat thermometer, if the juices run clear when the tip of a sharp knife is inserted into the thickest part of the body and there is no trace of pink in the meat.

TO MAKE THE GREEN BEAN SALAD:

When the chicken is nearly done, steam the green beans in a covered medium saucepan over a medium-high heat until tender, 10–12 minutes. While steaming, heat the olive oil in a small frying pan over a medium heat. Add the onions and fry until browned, 10–12 minutes. Add the vinegar, brown sugar, salt and pepper and stir well. Add the ham and cook for 3–4 minutes until heated through. Remove from heat and toss the ham and onion mixture with the green beans.

Leave the chicken to sit for 15–20 minutes before carving. Note: the chicken temperature will raise a few degrees while resting.

Serve the chicken, potatoes and green beans together.

'WELCOME. WELCOME. TO ANOTHER YEAR
AT HOGWARTS. NOW I'D LIKE TO SAY A FEW WORDS
BEFORE WE ALL BECOME TOO BEFUDDLED BY
OUR EXCELLENT FEAST.'

– Albus Dumbledore, *Harry Potter and the Prisoner of Azkaban*

NOTE

Place each potato on two chopsticks to help you not cut all the way
through the potatoes.

UNBEFUDDLED ROAST HAM WITH BUTTERED CREAMY MASHED POTATOES AND A HERBY HEAP OF PEAS

GF | Yield: 4 servings | Prep time: 30 minutes, plus 3 hours resting for the batter | Cook time: 2 hours

Although Hogwarts and the Great Hall were inspired by some of England's most historic buildings, they contain elements that are unique to the castle. These include gargoyles of the heraldic creatures representing the four houses: a lion (Gryffindor), snake (Slytherin), eagle (Ravenclaw) and badger (Hufflepuff). The figures hold flambeaux (bowls of flames) that light the hall along with the multitudes of floating candles.

The ceiling of the Great Hall portrays a magical sky that can be seen among the hammerbeam-style roof trusses, created through digital visual effects. 'You still want a hint that there's a roof there,' says visual effects producer Emma Norton, 'so you see the structure, almost like a ghost, through the sky.'

This classic recipe is inspired by one of the dishes at the first film's first feast: roast ham with pineapple and cherries, seen on Slytherin's table. It is served with mashed potatoes and peas, another English classic.

POTATOES

- 1.4kg Maris Piper potatoes, peeled and cut into 2.5cm cubes
- 55g unsalted butter, diced
- 60–75ml milk
- Salt
- Pepper

HAM

- 1 x 1kg small gammon joint
- 1 x 285–350g jar maraschino cherries
- 2 x 575g cans pineapple slices
- 30g unsalted butter
- 30g soft light brown sugar

TO MAKE THE POTATOES:

Bring a pot of water to the boil, and add the potatoes. Boil for 15–20 minutes or until tender. Remove from heat and drain. Then add the butter to the potatoes, spreading it out over the surface. Cover the pot and let sit for 5 minutes. Use a potato masher to mash the potatoes to your desired texture. Add the milk (more for creamier potatoes) and salt and pepper to taste. Stir well. Cover until ready to serve.

TO MAKE THE HAM:

About 2 hours before dinner, place the gammon in a large stockpot and cover in cold water. Bring to a boil, reduce the heat and simmer for 30 minutes per 500g until cooked through – the juices should run clear when a skewer is inserted into the thickest part of the meat. Remove the ham from the water. Lift off the skin with a sharp knife and discard.

Preheat the oven to 180°C/160°C fan/Gas Mark 4. Line a baking sheet with foil. Place the ham on the foil. Use cocktail sticks to secure cherries in the centre of pineapple slices all over the ham (they should touch). The cherries will hold the pineapple in place.

In a small saucepan, melt the butter over a medium heat. Stir in the brown sugar. Brush half of the mixture all over the ham. Place the ham in the oven and bake for 20 minutes. Remove from the oven and brush with the remaining mixture. (Tip: reheat the butter mixture for easier brushing.) Bake the ham for 20 minutes more.

PEAS

300g frozen peas

30g unsalted butter

2 cloves garlic, very finely chopped

1 teaspoon chopped fresh thyme

1 teaspoon chopped fresh rosemary

Salt (optional)

Pepper (optional)

TO MAKE THE PEAS:

Steam the peas in a small covered saucepan over a medium-high heat for 5–6 minutes until tender. In a small frying pan over a medium heat, melt the butter. Add the garlic and cook for 1–2 minutes or until fragrant. Pour the butter mixture over the drained peas and add the thyme and rosemary. Toss well. Season with salt and pepper, if desired.

Slice the ham. Serve with the peas and mashed potatoes. Leftover ham should be stored in an airtight container in the refrigerator and consumed within 5 days.

✦ **BEHIND THE MAGIC** ✦

The Great Hall hosts a number of skies: moonlit clouds, falling snow and Emma Watson's (Hermione) personal favourite: a depiction of the cosmos seen in *Harry Potter and the Prisoner of Azkaban* that she calls 'brilliant'.

'FIRST, I'M PLEASED TO WELCOME PROFESSOR R.J. LUPIN, WHO HAS KINDLY CONSENTED TO FILL THE POST OF DEFENCE AGAINST THE DARK ARTS. GOOD LUCK TO YOU, PROFESSOR.'

– Albus Dumbledore, *Harry Potter and the Prisoner of Azkaban*

END-OF-YEAR FEAST BEEF SHORT RIBS WITH YORKSHIRE PUDDING AND BUTTERY DICED CARROTS

YIELD: 4 servings | PREP TIME: 30 minutes | Cook time: 8½ hours

---

The end of term at Hogwarts brings a great feast and an awarding of the house cup, based on the points each house has accumulated throughout the year. Slytherin was ahead at the end of Harry's first year, in *Harry Potter and the Philosopher's Stone*, until Headmaster Dumbledore awarded additional points to Hermione, Ron, Harry and Neville, bringing the win to Gryffindor.

Four hourglass-shaped cylinders for keeping track of the points were mounted to the wall of the Great Hall behind the professors' table. Production designer Stuart Craig used tens of thousands of glass beads in the house colours, causing a national shortage of beads in England that year.

These beef short ribs are cooked in a slow cooker, served with a classic English Yorkshire pudding and accompanied by delicious diced carrots. Fifty points to your house for a winning feast!

SHORT RIBS
900g boneless short ribs

1 teaspoon coarse salt

1 teaspoon pepper

350ml beef stock

300ml red wine

1 tablespoon soy sauce

1 tablespoon Worcestershire sauce

1 teaspoon garlic powder

1 teaspoon onion granules

1 teaspoon dried rosemary

TO MAKE THE SHORT RIBS:

Season the short ribs all over with salt and pepper. Heat a large frying pan over a high heat. Add the short ribs (do not crowd them – you may need to cook them in more than one batch), and sear for 1 minute on each side. Transfer to a slow cooker. Continue until all the short ribs have been seared. Reserve any of the fat from the pan in a small jug and set aside for the Yorkshire pudding.

Add the beef stock, red wine, soy sauce, Worcestershire sauce, garlic powder, onion granules and rosemary to the slow cooker. Set the heat to low and leave to cook for about 8 hours. The ribs should be fall-apart tender.

Continued on page 141

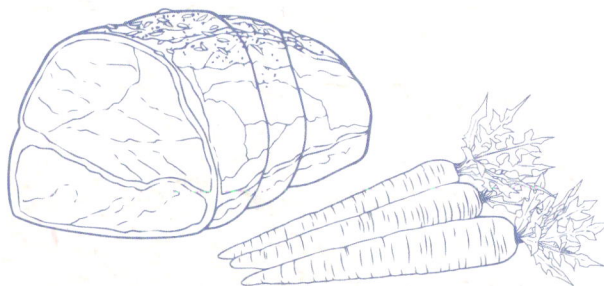

Continued from page 138

YORKSHIRE PUDDING
4 medium eggs

125g plain flour

175ml milk

½ teaspoon salt

1 tablespoon water

60ml rapeseed oil or
    50g bacon fat or lard

CARROTS
675g carrots, diced

30g unsalted butter

Salt

Pepper

★ **BEHIND THE MAGIC** ★

Before each film began, the house points beads were moved to the top of each cylinder. After all, no points had been awarded yet.

TO MAKE THE YORKSHIRE PUDDING:

In a medium mixing bowl, whisk together the eggs, flour, milk, salt and water until smooth. Transfer to an airtight container and chill in the refrigerator for at least 3 hours.

During the last 30 minutes of cooking the ribs, preheat the oven to 230°C/210°C fan/Gas Mark 8 and add more oil or fat to the reserved drippings from the frying pan to make 60ml. Fill each of 12 holes of a muffin tin with 1 teaspoon of the drippings. Place the muffin tin in the oven and heat for 7–8 minutes. Remove from the oven and divide the Yorkshire pudding batter evenly among the holes.

Bake for 15 minutes or until the puddings are puffed and golden.

TO MAKE THE CARROTS:

When the short ribs are nearly done, place the carrots into a medium saucepan with about 2.5cm of water (use a steaming insert if you like, but it is okay if you do not have one). Cook over a medium-high heat for 10–15 minutes. Drain. Melt the butter in a small frying pan over a medium heat, allowing it to continue cooking until it begins to brown. Toss with the carrots. Season with salt and pepper to taste.

Serve the short ribs, Yorkshire pudding and carrots together. These can be served on a plate (arranged) or in separate serving platters.

OVEN METHOD FOR SHORT RIBS:

Preheat the oven to 160°C/140°C fan/Gas Mark 3.

Season the short ribs with the salt and pepper. Place a large casserole over a medium-high heat on the hob and add 1 tablespoon vegetable oil. Sear the short ribs, in batches if necessary, until it is all well browned. Remove the meat from the pot and set aside. Add the red wine, stock, Worcestershire sauce and soy sauce to the pot, using it to deglaze the bits on the bottom. Add the garlic powder, onion granules and rosemary and stir to combine. Add the beef back in, ensuring it is submerged in the liquid. Cover and place in the oven. Cook for 2½–3 hours or until the meat is tender and falls apart. Serve with the juices.

To use the beef fat for your Yorkshire pudding and make a more traditional gravy, transfer the meat to a platter, cover with foil and set aside. Use a fat separator to separate the fat from the stock. Use the beef fat as the drippings for the puddings. To make the gravy, add the stock to a saucepan over a medium heat and reduce down until it coats the back of a spoon. A bit of tapioca starch can be added if desired.

'ANOTHER YEAR HAS GONE. AND NOW AS I UNDERSTAND IT. THE HOUSE CUP NEEDS AWARDING.'

– Albus Dumbledore, *Harry Potter and the Philosopher's Stone*

THE GREY LADY'S FINGERLING POTATOES WITH PANCETTA AND RED ONIONS

GF | YIELD: 4 servings | PREP TIME: 15 minutes | COOK TIME: 20 minutes

---

The Grey Lady, the ghost of Ravenclaw house, first appears in *Harry Potter and the Philosopher's Stone*, attired in a late Renaissance–era dress with a fitted bodice and bell-shape skirt. She also materializes in *Harry Potter and the Chamber of Secrets* in the Gryffindor common room, oddly enough, until Harry politely suggests that she is disturbing him. Her true identity – Helena Ravenclaw, the daughter of house founder Rowena Ravenclaw – is revealed in *Harry Potter and the Deathly Hallows – Part 2*, when Luna Lovegood informs Harry that he must speak with her as he searches for the Ravenclaw diadem Horcrux. The Grey Lady was recast for her more prominent role in the final film and was reimagined wearing simpler clothes that are more medieval in style. The fitted dress has an embroidered undergown and a laced overgown with long, draping sleeves.

The identity of the Grey Lady and the location of the diadem may be a challenge for Harry to solve, but there's no mystery here: These boiled fingerling potatoes, finished in a pan with pancetta and onions, are melt-in-your-mouth good.

675g fingerling potatoes

2 tablespoons olive oil

115g pancetta, cubed

½ small red onion, diced

2 tablespoons red wine vinegar

½ teaspoon Dijon mustard

Salt

Pepper

Place the fingerling potatoes in a large saucepan with about 2.5cm of water. Cover and cook over a medium-high heat for 13–16 minutes or until tender. Remove from the heat, drain and slice in half on a chopping board. Set aside.

In a large frying pan over a medium heat, warm 1 tablespoon olive oil. Add the pancetta and red onion and cook until the onion is tender, 5–7 minutes.

Add the potatoes to the frying pan. Cook, stirring occasionally, until the potatoes begin to brown, 7–8 minutes. Remove from heat.

In a small mixing bowl, whisk together the red wine vinegar, the remaining 1 tablespoon olive oil, the mustard and salt and pepper to taste. Pour over the potatoes and toss well.

Serve warm with a sandwich, such as Surbiton Smoked Ham Toasties (see page 40).

✦ BEHIND THE MAGIC ✦

The Grey Lady is also seen in *Harry Potter and the Chamber of Secrets* taking notes at one of the desks in Professor McGonagall's Transfiguration class.

'YOU'RE THE GREY LADY, THE GHOST OF RAVENCLAW TOWER.'
'I DO NOT ANSWER TO THAT NAME.'

– Harry Potter and Helena Ravenclaw,
Harry Potter and the Deathly Hallows – Part 2

SORTING HAT CEREMONY PEAS, BACON AND DICED ONIONS

GF | YIELD: 4 servings | PREP TIME: 10 minutes | COOK TIME: 25 minutes

---

Before the school year's opening feast in the Great Hall, first-year students are sorted into one of four Hogwarts houses: Gryffindor, Hufflepuff, Ravenclaw or Slytherin. During Harry Potter's years at Hogwarts, Professor Minerva McGonagall places the Sorting Hat upon the student's head and the hat then declares their house.

The Sorting Hat, originally created as a suede hat by costume designer Judianna Makovsky, was both a practical and a digital construction. Seven Sorting Hats were made for practical use, based on the 'master hat' in *Harry Potter and the Philosopher's Stone*. First, leather material was rolled into a cone form and soaked in hot water. Then it was squashed down upon itself and left overnight on a heating unit. Once the hat was dry, it was dyed, aged and imprinted lightly with Celtic symbols. You would never know each of the hats had different wrinkles and blemishes because they are never seen together.

Serving this tasty pea-based side dish, flavoured with fried bacon and onions, would be the easiest decision the Sorting Hat could make (as if the Sorting Hat would be asked to choose a side dish!); it will complement any main dish on the table.

- 115g bacon, chopped
- 1 medium brown onion, finely diced
- 300g frozen peas
- 1 tablespoon cider vinegar
- Salt
- Pepper

In a large frying pan over a medium heat, cook the bacon until browned, 7–9 minutes. Transfer the bacon to a kitchen paper–lined plate, leaving the bacon grease in the pan. Add the onion and fry for 10 minutes or until softened. Add the peas, vinegar and salt and pepper to taste to the pan. Cook, stirring occasionally, for 5 minutes or until heated through. Stir in the bacon.

These peas are delicious served with Diagon Alley Steak and Ale Pie (see page 33).

★ BEHIND THE MAGIC ★

Production designer Stuart Craig was very impressed with the Sorting Hat. 'It's really quite ingenious,' he said, 'the way that the eyes and mouth are just parts of its folds.'

'WHEN I CALL YOUR NAME, YOU WILL COME FORTH. I SHALL PLACE THE SORTING HAT ON YOUR HEAD, AND YOU WILL BE SORTED INTO YOUR HOUSES.'

– Minerva McGonagall, *Harry Potter and the Philosopher's Stone*

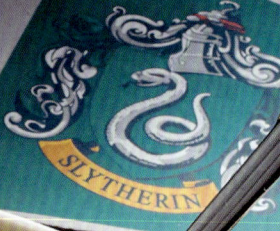

THE BLOODY BARON'S MUSHROOMS WITH GARLIC BUTTER

V, GF | YIELD: 4 servings | PREP TIME: 10 minutes | COOK TIME: 15 minutes

---

Each house at Hogwarts has its own resident ghost, and Slytherin's is the Bloody Baron. He makes his presence known at the start-of-term feast in *Harry Potter and the Philosopher's Stone* by swooping in through the walls of the Great Hall, swooshing and swashing his sword as he flies over Slytherin's table. The actors who played the Hogwarts house ghosts were hooked on to wires and lifted 6.5 metres in the air to film their entrances into the Great Hall.

Each ghost represented a different timeline: The Bloody Baron was dressed in the Rococo period of the early 1700s. 'I didn't want them to look like your traditional ghosts, with chiffon waving all over the place,' says costume designer Judianna Makovsky. 'I wanted real clothes from a real period.'

A traditional dish as old as the Bloody Baron himself, this lush, fragrant dish will easily make its presence known at your table, with no need for swooshing or swooping. Here, chestnut mushrooms are fried until tender and then bathed in a garlic butter sauce with white wine, a side that the Bloody Baron would have loved before his untimely passing.

- 1 tablespoon olive oil
- 30g unsalted butter, diced
- 350g whole chestnut mushrooms, quartered
- ¼ teaspoon pepper
- 1 teaspoon salt
- 4 cloves garlic, very finely chopped
- 60ml white wine
- 1 tablespoon chopped fresh parsley

Heat the olive oil and butter in a large frying pan over a medium-high heat. When the butter foams, add the mushrooms and season with pepper. Cook, stirring occasionally, for 5–7 minutes or until the mushrooms are browned. Add the salt and continue to cook until the mushrooms have released their juices.

Add the garlic and cook for 2–3 minutes until fragrant. Pour in the white wine and cook, stirring occasionally, until the liquid has evaporated, 4–5 minutes.

Remove from heat and toss with the parsley before serving. These mushrooms are delicious with the Room of Requirement Meatballs in Red Wine Sauce (see page 70).

✦ BEHIND THE MAGIC ✦

The Bloody Baron wears breeches and a waistcoat, with a decorative sash across his outercoat featuring the bloodstain that seemingly gives the ghost his name.

'LOOK. IT'S THE BLOODY BARON!'

– Slytherin Girl, *Harry Potter and the Philosopher's Stone*

THE FAT FRIAR'S GARLIC AND PARSLEY ROASTED PARSNIPS

V, V+, GF | YIELD: 4 servings | PREP TIME: 15 minutes | COOK TIME: 15 minutes

When the Fat Friar, the ghost of Hufflepuff house, enters the Great Hall at the start-of-term feast in *Harry Potter and the Philosopher's Stone*, he does not swoop in from the walls or ceiling like the other ghosts – he flies up from the floor, waving a tankard and whooping with glee.

'We were flying!' says Simon Fisher-Becker, who plays the Fat Friar. 'It was a wonderful experience.' Because the Fat Friar had only a few seconds of screen time, Fisher-Becker joked that his name in the credits is on the screen longer than he was.

Like the Fat Friar's appearance in the Great Hall, this dish may last on your table for only a short time because it is so delicious. An indulgent vegetable side that could have been found among the list of recipes the Fat Friar left the school cooks, this recipe calls for piquant parsnips to be cut into thick matchstick-sized pieces and roasted in a mixture of oil, garlic, salt and pepper.

- 450g parsnips, peeled
- 2 tablespoons olive oil
- Salt and pepper
- 2 cloves garlic, very finely chopped
- 1–2 tablespoons very finely chopped fresh parsley

Cut the parsnips into 5cm pieces, and then cut them into 5mm-thick matchsticks. It is essential that they are evenly cut.

Heat the olive oil in a large frying pan over a medium heat. Once the oil is hot, add the parsnips and season them with a couple pinches of salt and pepper. Cook, stirring occasionally, for 10–12 minutes or until they begin to brown.

Add the garlic to the pan and toss well. Season with more salt and pepper to taste. Cook, stirring, for a further 2–3 minutes until the garlic is fragrant and the parsnips are tender.

Remove from heat and toss with parsley. Taste and adjust the seasoning as desired. These are delicious served with The Burrow Meat Slices (see page 41).

✶ BEHIND THE MAGIC ✶

As member of a charitable order, the Fat Friar was dressed in simple grey robes.

'WHOO HOO HOO!'

– The Fat Friar, *Harry Potter and the Philosopher's Stone*

FLOATING CANDLES HERB BUTTER-BRUSHED CORN ON THE COB

V, GF | YIELD: 4 servings | PREP TIME: 5 minutes | COOK TIME: 15 minutes

---

Beneath a magical ceiling in the Great Hall float hundreds of candles. For *Harry Potter and the Philosopher's Stone*, 'We had 370 real candles, all floating up and down on wires at different times,' says special effects supervisor John Richardson. 'It looked really magical.' Director Chris Columbus remembers the very first shot of the Great Hall: '[We] craned down through the floating candles. You couldn't see anything holding them up.' However, the flames caused the wires to break, so for safety reasons, the real candles were switched to digital versions. Five sizes of CGI candles were created, with varied flame cycles so that no two candles looked alike. Going digital also allowed for unique arrangements, with candles set in circles, spirals and even starfish shapes.

Much like the Great Hall's floating candles, these golden ears of corn are cut down into smaller pieces and brushed with a flavourful herb butter seasoning that elevates them to a buttery, herby, well-seasoned treat that will light up your tables when served.

- 4 frech corn cobs, husks removed
- 45g unsalted butter
- ½ teaspoon dried thyme
- ½ teaspoon dried rosemary
- ½ teaspoon paprika
- ½ teaspoon garlic powder
- ½ teaspoon coarse salt

Cut each corn cob into 3 even pieces.

Bring a pot of water to the boil (you will need enough water to cover the corn once it is added). Add the corn and cook until tender, about 10 minutes.

Meanwhile, melt the butter in a small saucepan over a medium heat. Remove from heat and add the thyme, rosemary, paprika, garlic powder and salt. Stir well to combine.

Arrange the cooked corn on a platter. Use a pastry brush to liberally coat each piece with the butter mixture and serve immediately. This is delightful served with Professor Slughorn's Dinner Party Sausage Rolls (see page 62).

✷ BEHIND THE MAGIC ✷

Dame Maggie Smith (Professor McGonagall) remembers walking into the Great Hall when the real candles were there. 'It was just amazing,' she says. 'It's a magic place to be.'

'WE'RE READY FOR YOU NOW. FOLLOW ME.'

– Minerva McGonagall, *Harry Potter and the Philosopher's Stone*

NEARLY HEADLESS NICK'S ROASTED PARMESAN AND ROSEMARY CAULIFLOWER AND BROCCOLI

V*, GF | YIELD: 4 servings | PREP TIME: 15 minutes | COOK TIME: 45 minutes

As Ron Weasley digs into a platter of drumsticks at the start-of-term feast in *Harry Potter and the Philosopher's Stone*, he is startled by the appearance of Sir Nicholas de Mimsy-Porpington, the resident ghost of Gryffindor house. Sir Nicholas is also known as Nearly Headless Nick, a nickname based on the result of a botched execution.

To emphasize his nearly headlessness, costume designer Judianna Makovsky dressed the ghost in a combination of Jacobean- and Elizabethan-style breeches and doublet, topped with a thin ruff. Makovsky remembers a lot of laughter during her costume fitting with actor John Cleese. 'And he let me go to town, willing to wear it all, including some ridiculous pumpkin hose.'

Cauliflower and broccoli florets are tossed with olive oil, rosemary, salt and pepper in this recipe and then finished off with Parmesan cheese. There is nothing 'nearly' here – it is a completely wonderful side dish.

1 head cauliflower, broken into small florets

2 tablespoons olive oil

1 teaspoon dried rosemary

1 teaspoon coarse salt

½ teaspoon pepper

150g broccoli florets

45g Parmesan cheese, grated

Preheat the oven to 200°C/180°C fan/Gas Mark 6. Line a baking sheet with foil.

In a large mixing bowl, toss the cauliflower florets with 1 tablespoon olive oil and the rosemary, salt and pepper. Spread the mixture on to the prepared baking sheet and place in the oven. Bake for 20 minutes.

Remove the baking sheet from the oven. In a large mixing bowl, toss the broccoli with the remaining tablespoon of olive oil, add to the cauliflower and stir to combine. Return to the oven and bake for 15 minutes.

Scatter the cauliflower and broccoli with the Parmesan cheese. Stir well to coat. Bake for 5–8 minutes or until the cheese begins to brown.

This is delightful served with The Burrow Meat Pie (see page 41).

(see page 41)

✳ BEHIND THE MAGIC ✳

To add to their otherworldly attributes, the ghosts were given a digital glow and trails of ghostly matter in post-production.

'NEARLY HEADLESS?
HOW CAN YOU BE NEARLY HEADLESS?'

– Hermione Granger, *Harry Potter and the Philosopher's Stone*

✳ NOTE

This recipe is fully vegetarian by omitting the Parmesan cheese.

ARGUS FILCH AND MRS NORRIS'S ROASTED GARLIC MASHED BUTTERNUT SQUASH

V, V+, GF | YIELD: 4 servings | PREP TIME: 10 minutes | COOK TIME: 1 hour

---

Argus Filch is the caretaker of both Hogwarts castle and its professors. With the help of his cat, Mrs Norris, he excels at tracking down students who are doing something they are not supposed to be doing. Filch and his cat are clearly devoted to each other. 'He not only worships Mrs Norris,' says David Bradley (Filch), '[but] he depends on her as his chief spy.'

Mrs Norris was played by several tabby Maine coon cats throughout the course of the films, and each was skilled at different behaviours. One cat, Max, was good at jumping up on Bradley and sitting on his shoulder, as in *Harry Potter and the Order of the Phoenix*. Another cat's talent was to rest in Bradley's arm; this cat also enjoyed a waltz at the Yule Ball in *Harry Potter and the Goblet of Fire*. Because the stone floors of the Great Hall were often chilly, whenever Mrs Norris was there, they were heated to keep her warm and comfortable.

This recipe, with butternut squash and roasted garlic mashed together with salt, pepper, paprika and thyme, is also warm and comforting. It's a delicious purr-éed side dish.

- 1 whole butternut squash
- 3 teaspoons olive oil
- Salt
- Pepper
- 1 head garlic
- ½ teaspoon paprika
- ½ teaspoon dried thyme
- 1 tablespoon chopped fresh parsley (optional)

Preheat the oven to 200°C/180°C fan/Gas Mark 6. Line a baking sheet with foil.

Cut off the stalk end of the butternut squash, then cut the squash in half lengthways down the centre. Use a spoon to scoop out the seeds and sinew threads from the two cavities; discard those parts.

Brush the cut side of the butternut squash with olive oil, about 1 teaspoon for each half. Season liberally with salt and pepper and place on the prepared baking sheet, cut-side down.

Cut the top 5mm off the garlic. Place in a square of foil and drizzle with the remaining 1 teaspoon olive oil. Season with salt and pepper to taste. Wrap in the foil and place on the baking sheet with the squash.

Roast for 50–60 minutes until the squash is cooked through and browned. Remove from the oven and leave to cool for 10 minutes before scooping the butternut squash into a large mixing bowl. Unwrap the garlic and squeeze the roasted cloves into the bowl as well. (Tip: sometimes it is easier to remove the papery covering and gently place the individual cloves into the bowl.) Use a potato masher to thoroughly mash the squash and the garlic together. Add the paprika and thyme and stir well. Taste and season with salt and pepper, as desired.

Transfer to a serving bowl and scatter with the chopped parsley, if desired. Enjoy immediately. This is delightful served with Diagon Alley Steak and Ale Pie (see page 33).

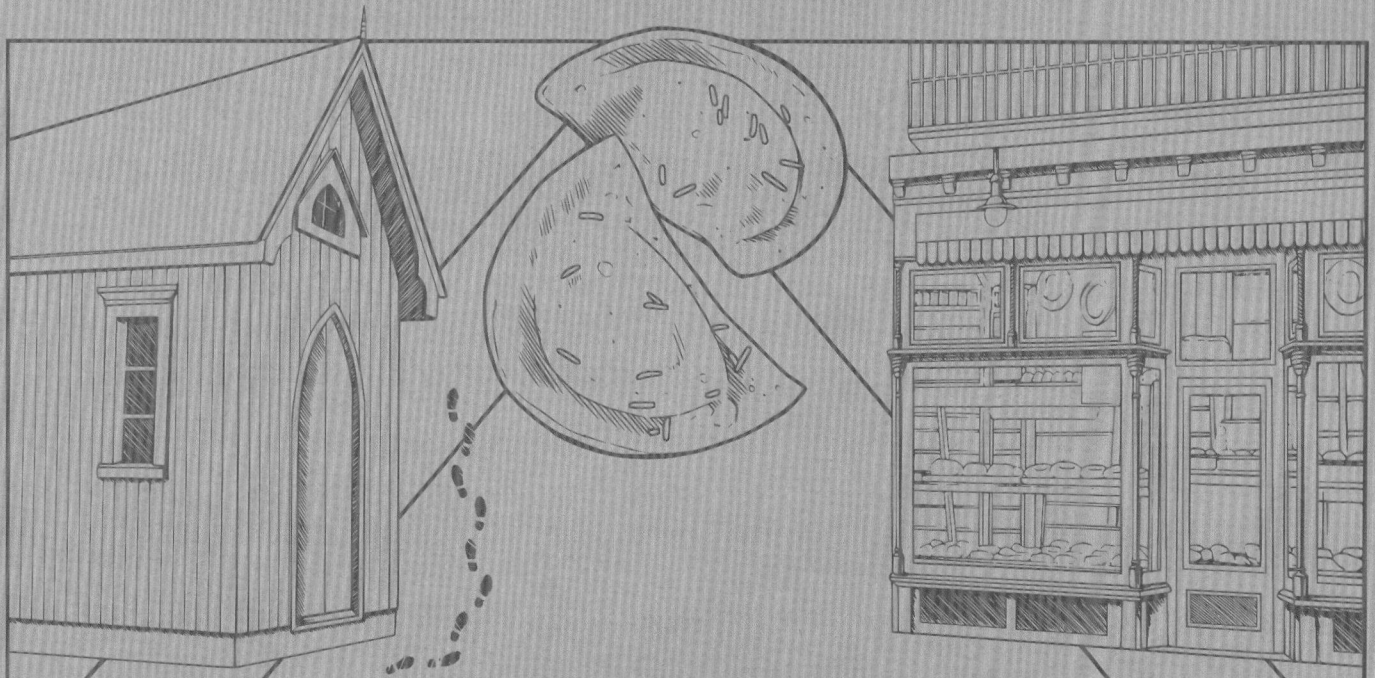

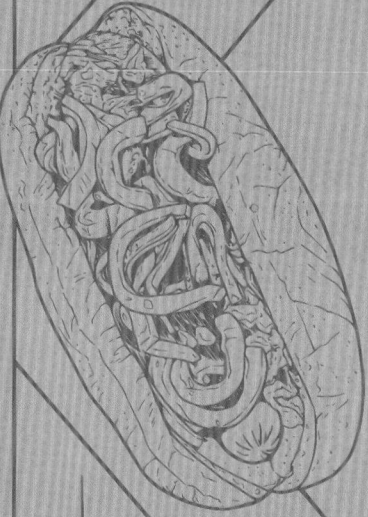

Chapter Four

NEW YORK CITY

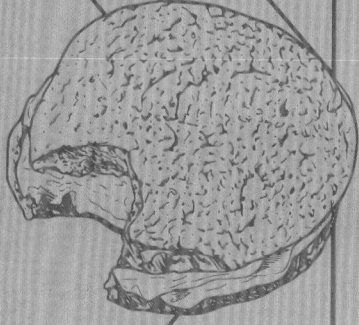

The AMER

SPELLBINDING SUMMER SIZZLERS!
Latest cuts straight from the Black Catwalk

FOR ALL AMERICAN WITCHES!

The **Witch's** FRIEND

SEPT 1926
2/5D

DISCOVER

New York

The **No-Maj Way!**

1925

TEDDY THE NIFFLER'S POUCH STUFFED TOMATOES

✳

V | YIELD: 4 servings | PREP TIME: 20 minutes | COOK TIME: 1 hour

---

When Newt Scamander arrives in New York City, he realizes that one of the latches on his case of beasts is faulty. One of his creatures, a Niffler, has managed to escape. Newt tracks the mischievous beast to Steen National Bank and corners him in the bank's basement vault. The Niffler, named Teddy, is opening the safe deposit boxes and stuffing their contents into the pouch on his tummy, for Nifflers will pursue anything shiny with tenacious determination.

To get Teddy to release his new treasures, Newt holds him upside down and tickles his tummy. Actor Eddie Redmayne (Newt) learned this technique after meeting with a zoologist who was working with a baby anteater. 'It would curl up into a little ball, and in order to make it relax, she would tickle his little belly,' he explains.

These baked tomatoes are stuffed with rice that's turned golden by saffron and topped with buttery Italian breadcrumbs. It is a golden culinary treasure that any Niffler would want to stuff into its pouch.

- 2 tablespoons olive oil
- 1 medium brown onion, finely chopped
- 185g basmati rice, rinsed
- ¼ teaspoon saffron threads
- 350ml vegetable stock
- ½ teaspoon salt
- 4 large tomatoes
- 50g Italian breadcrumbs
- 2 tablespoons unsalted butter, melted

Heat the olive oil in a medium pot over a medium heat. Add the onions and cook for 7–10 minutes or until they begin to brown.

Add the rice and stir well. Stir in the saffron, vegetable stock and salt. Bring to the boil and reduce heat to low. Cover and cook for 20 minutes without disturbing. Remove from heat and leave to sit for 10 minutes.

Preheat the oven to 190°C/170°C fan/Gas Mark 5.

Cut off the top 5mm of the tomatoes and scoop out the insides. Fill each tomato with rice, pressing it to fit inside. Place in a 20cm square glass baking dish.

In a small bowl, combine the breadcrumbs with the butter. Crumble and scatter evenly over the tomatoes.

Place the baking dish in the oven and bake for 20–25 minutes or until the breadcrumbs are browned. This is delightful served with Hermione Granger's Extension Charm Bacon and Potato Pasties (see page 22).

(see page 22)

✳ **BEHIND THE MAGIC** ✳

The Niffler was based on several creatures, including an anteater, a mole, a badger, a wallaby and a platypus, to make one cute, cuddly and unique beast.

'REALLY?!'
– Newt Scamander, *Fantastic Beasts and Where to Find Them*

NIFFLER BABIES' EVERYTHING CHICKEN WINGS

YIELD: 8 servings | PREP TIME: 15 minutes | COOK TIME: 40 minutes

Nifflers love anything shiny. They will pursue a coin, a bracelet or even a glittery button with the single-minded goal to acquire it and store it in a pouch on their tummy. To capture the stubbornness of Teddy the Niffler and the Niffler Babies – and to represent how the creatures miscalculate their ability to physically get what they want and miss the mark with a laughable clumsiness – the animators on the Fantastic Beasts films watched videos of animal 'fails'.

'The lovely thing about animals is their naivety,' says animation supervisor Pablo Grillo. 'They think if they stay still, you can't see them. The humour comes from Newt's and his Nifflers' past, and almost the respect Newt gives him for his skill. He admires it, but it's always getting them into problems.'

You won't fail with these crispy baked chicken wings, coated in an everything seasoning as a tribute to these adorable silky black creatures.

Ingredients

- Butter or oil, for greasing
- 95g plain flour
- 1 teaspoon coarse salt
- ½ teaspoon pepper
- 125ml rapeseed oil (plus more, as needed)
- 1.35kg chicken wings, with tips removed and pieces separated
- 35g mixed poppy and sesame seeds

Method

Preheat the oven to 220°C/200°C fan/Gas Mark 7. Line a baking sheet with foil and grease the foil.

Whisk together the flour, salt and pepper in a small mixing bowl. Place in a shallow bowl or a plate with a big lip. Place the oil in another bowl (add more as needed). Dip each chicken wing in the flour, flipping to coat on both sides, and then tap gently to remove any excess. Then dip each wing in the oil, turning gently to coat (do this pretty fast). Arrange on the prepared baking sheet. Repeat until all the wings have been coated.

Bake for 20 minutes. Use tongs to carefully flip all the wings. Bake for a further 20–22 minutes until the wings are golden on each side.

Place the mixed seeds in a large mixing bowl. Add the wings to the bowl, hot from the oven. Toss thoroughly. Enjoy immediately.

✶ BEHIND THE MAGIC ✶

Eddie Redmayne refers to Teddy the Niffler as 'the bane of Newt Scamander's life.'

'FOR THE LAST TIME, YOU PILFERING PEST – PAWS OFF WHAT DOESN'T BELONG TO YOU!'

– Newt Scamander, *Fantastic Beasts and Where to Find Them*

MACUSA CODFISH CAKES

GF | YIELD: 4 servings | PREP TIME: 20 minutes | COOK TIME: 35 minutes

---

MACUSA is the North American version of Great Britain's Ministry of Magic, created shortly after the Salem Witch Trials of the late 1600s. MACUSA's offices, where Tina takes Newt in *Fantastic Beasts and Where to Find Them*, are set in New York City's 1900s Gothic-style Woolworth building, which matches the architectural style of Hogwarts. Production designer Stuart Craig also believes the building was chosen because it has a large stone owl on its entrance arch.

To make MACUSA different and fresh, Craig decided to put the offices in the basement. 'And the further down you go, the more menial the work and the more dreadful the conditions,' he says. The Wand Permit Office, where Tina works, is on this lower level.

Cod is a staple of New England's fishing industry, fished out of ports such as Salem Harbor for hundreds of years. Cod, potatoes, onions, parsley and paprika combine in these fried fish cakes, served with a herby dill soured cream, for a North American classic.

CODFISH CAKES

2 large potatoes, peeled and cubed

1 teaspoon olive oil

450g cod fillets

2 medium eggs, beaten

15g butter

1 tablespoon onion granules

1 tablespoon chopped fresh parsley

1 teaspoon paprika

1 teaspoon salt

½ teaspoon pepper

3 tablespoons rapeseed oil

HERBY DILL SOURED CREAM

175g soured cream

55g mayonnaise

1 tablespoon very finely chopped fresh dill

2 teaspoons lemon juice

½ teaspoon salt

½ teaspoon garlic powder

Fresh black pepper

TO MAKE THE CODFISH CAKES:
Place the potatoes in a large pot with enough water to cover the potatoes; bring to the boil over a high heat. Reduce the heat to medium-low and simmer for about 15 minutes or until the potatoes are tender. Drain and add the potatoes to a large mixing bowl.

In a large frying pan, heat the olive oil over a medium heat. Add the cod and cook, flipping once, until it looks opaque throughout, 7–8 minutes total. Flake the cod into small pieces with a fork and add to the large mixing bowl. Leave to cool slightly.

Add the eggs, butter, onion, parsley, paprika, salt and pepper. Mash together with a potato masher until well combined.

Heat the oil in a large frying pan over a medium heat.

Divide the mixture into small round balls, about 3 tablespoons each, and add to the frying pan, pressing slightly to flatten (leave the patties about 2cm thick). A large biscuit scoop can make quick work of this. Cook the patties until golden on both sides, flipping once, 4–6 minutes per side.

TO MAKE THE HERBY DILL SOURED CREAM:
In a small bowl, mix the soured cream, mayo, dill, lemon juice, salt and garlic powder; blend until smooth. Cover and refrigerate until ready to serve. Add pepper to taste right before serving.

KOWALSKI BAKERY'S FLUFFY CINNAMON BUNS WITH VANILLA BEAN GLAZE

✶

V | YIELD: 8 servings | PREP TIME: 30 minutes, plus 4 hours for rise | COOK TIME: 20 minutes

---

Actor Dan Fogler (Jacob Kowalski) feels it is kismet that he plays the part of a baker in the Fantastic Beasts films. 'I knew the character really well because my great-grandfather was a baker in the same area,' Fogler explains. 'He had the best pumpernickel in New York; that's what he was known for.' Fogler believes his family legacy contributed to him winning the part, supposing that the director and producers saw his audition tape and said, "Oh, this guy knows this character." Because he's very much in my blood.'

During a glimpse of Kowalski's Bakery, after Jacob secures a loan using the Occamy egg shells Newt has gifted him in *Fantastic Beasts and Where to Find Them*, we see shelves filled with breads and pastries, including cinnamon buns. This recipe offers oversized yeast-raised cinnamon buns filled with cinnamon and brown sugar, coated with a vanilla bean glaze.

CINNAMON BUNS

250ml milk

2 tablespoons caster sugar

1 teaspoon coarse salt

115g unsalted butter

2¼ teaspoons fast-action dried yeast

375g plain flour, plus more for dusting

100g soft light brown sugar

2 teaspoons cinnamon

GLAZE

125g icing sugar

45ml milk

1 teaspoon vanilla bean paste or vanilla extract

TO MAKE THE CINNAMON BUNS: scald the milk in a medium pot set over a medium heat – it should have tiny bubbles on the surface and be just short of boiling. Remove from heat and stir in the sugar, salt and 55g of the butter (cut into pieces). Once the butter is melted, stir until cooled to 43°C. Then sprinkle the yeast on the surface and leave to rest for 2–3 minutes until it is foamy.

Add the flour 125g at a time, stirring after each addition until combined. Turn out the dough on to a floured board and knead with floured hands until the dough forms a cohesive ball. Transfer to a large oiled bowl, cover with a tea towel and set in a warm, draught-free area for about 2 hours or until the dough has doubled in size.

Flour a work surface, turn out the dough and roll into a 20 x 15cm rectangle. Melt the remaining butter and brush the top of the dough all over with it. Scatter with the brown sugar and cinnamon, taking care to spread it to the edges. Roll from a long edge to create a cylinder.

Use a sharp knife to cut the dough into 8 equal pieces. Transfer to an oven-safe glass baking pan. Cover the pan with a tea towel, leaving room for the dough to rise, and leave to rise for 2 hours.

Preheat the oven to 200°C/180°C fan/Gas Mark 6. Remove the cover from the baking dish,and bake for 18–20 minutes or until golden. Remove from the oven and leave to cool while you prepare the glaze.

TO MAKE THE GLAZE: in a small bowl, add the icing sugar and milk. Add the vanilla bean paste or extract. Stir together to form the glaze. Drizzle all over the cinnamon buns. Serve immediately.

QUEENIE GOLDSTEIN'S APPLE ALMOND COFFEE CAKE

✳

V | YIELD: 1 coffee cake | PREP TIME: 20 minutes | COOK TIME: 30 minutes

The love story between the witch Queenie Goldstein and the No-Maj Jacob Kowalski is one of the sweetest in the wizarding world. 'Queenie loves Jacob,' says Alison Sudol. 'He loves to bake, and she loves to cook. He makes her laugh. He respects her.' Because Queenie is a Legilimens, 'She's able to see into him, sees how good he is through and through,' she continues. 'It's a lovely dynamic between the two of them that he can't hide from her – but he has nothing to hide, because even when he says something that he doesn't mean to, it's still great.'

Although we do not get to see Queenie making breakfast for Jacob because he disappears into Newt's case after they have had dinner the night before, we know that she makes a mean apple strudel, which is one of Jacob's favourites. This moist and tender crumble-topped New York coffee cake–inspired dish, featuring apples and almonds, would probably be something she would bake.

COFFEE CAKE

85g unsalted butter, cut into pieces, plus more for greasing

250g plain flour

2 teaspoons baking powder

1 teaspoon salt

100g sugar

50g flaked almonds

1 Granny Smith apple, peeled and finely diced

1 medium egg

150ml milk

1 teaspoon almond extract

TOPPING

45g unsalted butter, melted

25g plain flour

45ml clear honey

¼ cup flaked almonds

TO MAKE THE COFFEE CAKE:

Preheat the oven to 200°C/180°C fan/Gas Mark 6. Thoroughly grease a 23cm round cake tin.

In a large mixing bowl, sift together the flour, baking powder, salt and sugar. Add the butter and use a pastry cutter or two knives to cut in, continuing until coarse crumbs form. Stir in the almonds and apples.

In a small bowl, whisk together the egg, milk and almond extract until light and frothy, 2–3 minutes. Pour into the flour mixture and stir until well combined. The dough will be stiff, but keep stirring until it is all incorporated. Transfer the dough to the prepared cake tin and press into one even layer.

TO MAKE THE TOPPING:

In a small bowl, stir together the butter, flour, honey and almonds until combined. Crumble on to the top of the dough.

Place the coffee cake in the oven and bake for 20–25 minutes or until a skewer inserted into the centre comes out clean. Leave to cool for 5 minutes before loosening the cake from the tin and transferring to a serving plate. Serve immediately while warm or leave to cool before cutting.

> **'DON'T WORRY, HONEY. MOST GUYS THINK WHAT YOU WAS THINKING THE FIRST TIME THEY SEE ME.'**
>
> – Queenie Goldstein to Jacob Kowalski,
> *Fantastic Beasts and Where to Find Them*

TINA GOLDSTEIN'S ULTIMATE NEW YORK HOT DOG

✴

GF* | YIELD: 4 servings | PREP TIME: 25 minutes | COOK TIME: 30 minutes

In *Fantastic Beasts and Where to Find Them*, ex-Auror Tina Goldstein munches on a hot dog as she listens to a fiery speech by the leader of a fanatical antimagic group: the New Salem Philanthropic Society. Unknowingly, a glob of mustard is smeared on her lip, pointed out later as Tina Disapparates with Newt after she demands an explanation about his escaped Niffler.

The filmmakers took scouting trips to New York City with the idea of finding locations for the films. 'Alas, there is remarkably little of 1926 New York in New York today,' says producer David Heyman. 'So it was easier, more controllable, more manageable for us to build it on the backlot at Leavesden Studios.'

Hot dog vendors in New York City seem to be everywhere, offering a long-established array of toppings beyond mustard and ketchup. This hot dog is topped with homemade onion sauce, sauerkraut and American-style mustard – a classic New York City combination.

1 tablespoon rapeseed oil

2 medium brown onions, thinly sliced

125ml water

70g ketchup

¼ teaspoon salt

⅛ teaspoon cinnamon

FOR SERVING

4 American frankfurters, freshly heated

4 frankfurter buns

450g sauerkraut, heated

American-style mustard

Heat the oil in a large frying pan over a medium heat. Add the onions and fry until soft, 7–9 minutes. Add the water, ketchup, salt and cinnamon. Stir. Continue cooking, stirring occasionally, until the liquid is reduced by half, about 15 minutes. Remove from heat and cool.

To assemble the hot dogs, place one hot boiled hot dog in a bun; top with the onion sauce, sauerkraut and brown mustard. Repeat with all the hot dogs. Serve.

✴ **NOTE**

If you can't find classic American-style yellow mustard, you can use wholegrain mustard or dijon mustard instead.
This recipe is easily made gluten-free by using gluten-free hot dog buns.

'HOT DOG... AGAIN?'
'DON'T READ MY MIND!'

– Queenie and Tina Goldstein, *Fantastic Beasts and Where to Find Them*

✴ **BEHIND THE MAGIC** ✴

The New Salem Philanthropic Society, which Tina is listening to when Newt bumps into her, was created to seek out and destroy wizards and witches in New York City.

WEST 24TH STREET CHICKEN À LA KING

✴

YIELD: 4 servings | PREP TIME: 10 minutes | COOK TIME: 30 minutes

---

One of the first scenes Katherine Waterston and Alison Sudol shot together as the Goldstein sisters was when preparing dinner for new friends Newt and Jacob in their apartment on West 24th Street. 'What's so amazing and insane about working in film,' says Waterston, 'is that sometimes you've just met a person, and then you have to move together in a space as though you do it every day.' The actresses asked each other how would they prepare the room together? Whose chores are whose? Queenie cooks and bakes, while Tina sets the table with her wand.

Chicken à la King is a classic American dish that was possibly created in Brooklyn, where the Goldstein sisters live. Using cooked chicken for this recipe makes it come together pretty quickly. The dish features a sherry tarragon cream sauce, with diced chicken accompanied by sweet red peppers and earthy mushrooms. This is a dish that Queenie might magically assemble in their apartment and serve over egg noodles.

- 1 tablespoon olive oil
- 225g sliced mushrooms
- 1 medium brown onion, diced
- Salt
- Pepper
- 75g unsalted butter, cut into pieces
- 30g plain flour
- 125ml dry sherry
- 350ml chicken stock
- 250ml milk
- 125ml double cream
- 2 tablespoons chopped fresh tarragon
- 150g frozen peas
- 175g roasted red peppers, chopped
- 575g cooked chicken, such as from a rotisserie chicken, diced

FOR SERVING
Cooked egg noodles

Heat the oil in a large frying pan over a medium heat. Add the mushrooms and onion and cook 10–12 minutes, stirring occasionally, until soft. Season with a few pinches of salt and pepper.

Add the butter and allow to melt. Push the onions and mushrooms to the side and add the flour. Whisk the flour into the butter. Add the sherry and whisk together.

Add the chicken stock, milk, double cream and tarragon and stir well. Bring to the boil and then reduce heat to medium-low. Simmer for 3–5 minutes until thickened. Stir in the peas, roasted red peppers and chicken and stir well. Cook for a further 3–4 minutes until cooked through. Season with additional salt and pepper to taste.

Serve as desired, but over noodles is recommended.

> **'NOW. YOU NEED FOOD.'**
>
> – Queenie Goldstein, *Fantastic Beasts and Where to Find Them*

JACOB AND QUEENIE'S WEDDING DAY PIEROGIES

V | YIELD: 6 servings | PREP TIME: 1 hour | COOK TIME: 30 minutes

---

Fantastic Beasts: The Secrets of Dumbledore concludes with the wedding of a very nervous Jacob Kowalski and a very calm Queenie Goldstein.

The wedding scene reminded Dan Fogler of the final scene in *Fantastic Beasts and Where to Find Them*, where Queenie comes into his bakery after Jacob has been Obliviated and there is an obvious connection and a remembrance. 'They matched that scene beautifully,' says Fogler. In the third film, 'She was standing there with a big smile on her face, and I became a puddle,' he admits. 'The nostalgia of the first film and the chemistry they have was palpable.'

'There was a sense in the room of everybody going "Yeah",' says Alison Sudol. 'This is finally happening. They fought through impossible challenges, and they found each other.'

This pierogi recipe – possibly one made by Jacob's grandmother (like her paczkis) – is a filled Polish pasta with Cheddar cheese, spring onions and potatoes inside.

DOUGH

375g plain flour, plus more for dusting

175ml cold water

1 medium egg, beaten

45g unsalted butter, melted and cooled slightly

1 teaspoon salt

Butter or oil, for greasing

FILLING

675g russet potatoes

175g mature Cheddar cheese, grated

2 spring onions, thinly sliced

¼ teaspoon coarse salt

¼ teaspoon pepper

2 tablespoons milk

30g salted butter

Chives, for garnish

TO MAKE THE DOUGH:

In a large bowl, combine the flour, water, egg, butter and salt. Mix well to form a dough.

Flour a flat work surface and turn out the dough on to the surface. Knead the dough for 4–5 minutes or until smooth and pliable.

Place the dough in a large greased mixing bowl. Cover with a tea towel and leave to sit at room temperature for 1 hour.

TO MAKE THE FILLING:

Preheat the oven to 190°C/170°C fan/Gas Mark 5. Rinse the potatoes and stab them 2–3 times with a fork. Place on a baking sheet and bake for 45 minutes or until tender. Remove from the oven and leave to cool for 20 minutes.

Line a baking sheet with greaseproof paper. Set aside.

Cut the potatoes in half. Use a spoon to scoop the flesh into the bowl of a stand mixer or a large mixing bowl if using a hand mixer. Add the Cheddar cheese, spring onions, salt and pepper. Run the mixer on low for 30 seconds, then increase the speed to medium for 1 minute. Add the milk and mix on medium until combined. The filling should be very smooth.

Continued on page 174

MAINS

172

Continued from page 172

Flour a work surface. Remove half of the dough from the bowl and place on the floured surface. Use a rolling pin to roll it to a 3mm thickness. Then use a 7.5cm biscuit cutter to cut rounds.

Place 1 heaped tablespoon of filling into the centre of each round. Fold the dough over and pinch the edges closed. Place the pierogies on the prepared baking sheet so that they are not touching and continue until all the dough and filling is used.

Heat a large pot (at least 4 litres) of salted water to boiling over a high heat. Reduce the heat to medium and add the pierogies in batches. Cook for 2–4 minutes or until they float. Remove with a slotted spoon.

In a small frying pan over a medium heat, melt the salted butter. Continue cooking until the butter begins to turn golden. Remove from heat and drizzle over the pierogies. Season with a pinch of salt and pepper. Sprinkle with snipped chives for garnish, if desired.

'ALBERT! DON'T FORGET THE PIEROGIES!'

– Jacob Kowalski, *Fantastic Beasts: The Secrets of Dumbledore*

HENRY SHAW JR'S SENATE RUN POTATO HOLLANDAISE

★

V, GF | YIELD: 4 servings | PREP TIME: 20 minutes | COOK TIME: 45 minutes

---

In *Fantastic Beasts and Where to Find Them*, *Clarion* newspaper publisher Henry Shaw holds a fund-raising dinner at City Hall to support his son's re-election campaign for the Senate. The white-tie affair is attended by the moneyed elite of New York City.

The New York City Hall that houses Shaw's campaign dinner was shot in St George's Hall in Liverpool, England. American flag buntings were hung around the room, with a centre point that had a huge hand-painted portrait of Senator Shaw. 'It looked amazing,' says Josh Cowdery, who plays Henry Shaw Jr. 'All that detail made it easier to feel like I was giving a real speech. If it was just a green screen and five guys in front of me, where everything would be added later, that would have been tough.'

This classic dish might be found on the menus of fancy New York restaurants in the 1920s and served at events like Shaw's campaign dinner. It is a great candidate for a side dish: simple, creamy and warming.

POTATOES

675g fingerling potatoes

2 cloves garlic, very finely chopped

1 teaspoon coarse salt

½ teaspoon pepper

2 tablespoons olive oil

HOLLANDAISE SAUCE

1 medium egg yolk

1 tablespoon lemon juice

¼ teaspoon salt

55g unsalted butter, melted

TO MAKE THE POTATOES:

Preheat the oven to 190°C/170°C fan/Gas Mark 5. Line a baking sheet with heavy-duty foil.

Slice the fingerling potatoes in half lengthways and place in a large mixing bowl. Season with garlic, salt and pepper. Drizzle with the olive oil. Stir vigorously until evenly coated.

Pour the potatoes on to the baking sheet in a single layer. Place in the oven and bake for 30–35 minutes or until browned and fork-tender, stirring once or twice during baking to prevent sticking. Remove from the oven and transfer to a serving dish.

TO MAKE THE HOLLANDAISE SAUCE:

In a small bowl, combine the egg yolk, lemon juice and salt. Whisk vigorously until blended, about 2 minutes. Drizzle in the melted butter in a slow, steady stream, whisking constantly. Taste and adjust the seasoning as desired.

★ **BEHIND THE MAGIC** ★

Hundreds of extras were dressed in vintage costumes for the campaign dinner. The Shaws arrived in a 1926 Phantom I Rolls-Royce.

'NOW. TONIGHT'S KEYNOTE SPEAKER NEEDS NO INTRODUCTION FROM ME. HE'S BEEN MENTIONED AS A FUTURE PRESIDENT – AND IF YOU DON'T BELIEVE ME. JUST READ HIS DADDY'S NEWSPAPER – LADIES AND GENTLEMEN. I GIVE YOU THE SENATOR FOR NEW YORK. HENRY SHAW!'

– Announcer, *Fantastic Beasts and Where to Find Them*

MOONCALF MOON CAKE SANDWICHES

V | YIELD: 6 servings | PREP TIME: 15 minutes | COOK TIME: 25 minutes
---

When Newt and Jacob go inside Newt's case of beasts in *Fantastic Beasts and Where to Find Them*, the Magizoologist asks Jacob to help him by feeding a herd of adorable Mooncalves. 'They're bizarre creatures that can only look up,' says visual effects supervisor Christian Manz, who suggested that the pellets Jacob feeds them should float 'so he can feed them like fish.'

Fortunately, Newt has rigged a moon above their environment, to attract the gaze of the Mooncalves' huge, round eyes on the top of their heads. Concept artist Dermot Power made it look as if the 'moon' Newt created had dropped, broke and was then reassembled: After all, Newt did not consider himself a perfect 'world builder.'

This recipe is a tribute to the Mooncalves' love of moonlight. These moon cakes feature a creamy filling between two soft biscuits. Two additional options for the velvety filling suggest adding peanut butter or chocolate.

BISCUITS
200g granulated sugar

115g unsalted butter, softened

2 medium egg yolks

250g plain flour

30g cocoa powder

1 teaspoon baking powder

1 teaspoon bicarbonate of soda

½ teaspoon salt

250ml milk

1 teaspoon vanilla extract

TO MAKE THE BISCUITS:

Preheat the oven to 180°C/160°C fan/Gas Mark 4. Line two large baking sheets with baking paper.

In the bowl of a stand mixer fitted with the paddle attachment, or a large mixing bowl if using a hand mixer, beat the sugar, butter and egg yolks on medium speed for about 2 minutes or until light and fluffy.

In a separate large mixing bowl, sift together the flour, cocoa powder, baking powder, bicarbonate of soda and salt.

With the mixer running on its lowest setting, add a little of the flour mixture and then a little of the milk, alternating between the two until all has been added. Add the vanilla extract and mix briefly to combine.

Use a large biscuit scoop (45ml capacity) to drop the dough in mounds on to the prepared baking sheet, leaving 5cm between them. This should make 16 biscuits.

Bake for 10–15 minutes or until set. Remove to a wire rack and cool completely.

Continued on page 179

Continued from page 176

FILLING

- 225g unsalted butter, softened
- 125g icing sugar
- 2 cups marshmallow creme
- 1 teaspoon vanilla extract
- Piping bag with a large star nozzle (optional)

TO MAKE THE FILLING:

Once the biscuits have cooled, add the butter, sugar, marshmallow creme and vanilla extract to the clean bowl of the stand mixer fitted with the whisk attachment, or a clean large mixing bowl if using a hand mixer; beat for 2–3 minutes or until light and fluffy. Divide evenly among 6 of the biscuits, with a spatula or using the piping bag and star nozzle. Top each with a second biscuit.

VARIATIONS

Peanut Butter Filling: add 125g peanut butter to the filling mixture when adding it to the mixing bowl. Beat as directed.

Chocolate Filling: add 20g cocoa powder and 1 tablespoon milk to the filling mixture when adding it to the mixing bowl. Beat as directed.

> 'ACTUALLY. WOULD YOU MIND THROWING SOME OF THESE PELLETS IN WITH THE MOONCALVES OVER THERE?'
>
> – Newt Scamander to Jacob Kowalski, *Fantastic Beasts and Where to Find Them*

THE BLIND PIG LAUGHING LEMONADE COCKTAILS

V, V+, GF | YIELD: 4 servings | PREP TIME: 1 hour | COOK TIME: 15 minutes

---

To help Newt locate his remaining escaped creatures, Tina Goldstein brings him, Jacob and Queenie to The Blind Pig, a speakeasy owned by Gnarlak. This cigar-chomping goblin was an informant of Tina's when she was an Auror. 'It's a dive bar,' says visual effects supervisor Christian Manz. 'We've got a goblin jazz band and jazz singer, a house-elf barman and house-elf waiters. We've got lots of moving Wanted posters everywhere, magical gambling going on, plus all the drinks. For me, it's one of the moments in the film where you really feel the 1920s.'

This Laughing Lemonade Cocktail is inspired by the Gigglewater Queenie orders at The Blind Pig. Jacob tries to drink it with a serious demeanour that lasts about 1 second before he emits a raucous, high-pitched giggle. A special simple syrup turns the homemade lemonade, ginger and vodka mix an unexpected colour that will bring smiles all around.

- 1 litre water
- 225g red cabbage, leaves torn
- 1 x 10cm-long piece ginger, peeled and thinly sliced
- 200g caster sugar
- ¼ teaspoon gold lustre dust (optional)
- 175ml vodka
- 4 large lemon wedges
- 125ml freshly squeezed lemon juice

In a saucepan, combine the water, cabbage leaves, ginger and sugar. Bring to the boil over a high heat and boil until the sugar is dissolved, about 5 minutes; then infuse for 10 minutes. Strain the liquid into a jar or jug, discarding the solids; chill in the refrigerator for 1 hour. If using the lustre dust, stir in before chilling and stir to redistribute before serving.

To serve: fill 4 glasses with ice and divide the purple-ginger mixture and the vodka evenly among the glasses. Garnish each glass with a lemon wedge. Guests can watch the transformation as they squeeze the lemon into their drink. Put the lemon juice in a jug so guests can add more lemon to taste.

> **'HOW DO I GET A DRINK IN THIS JOINT?'**
>
> – Jacob Kowalski, *Fantastic Beasts and Where to Find Them*

★ **BEHIND THE MAGIC** ★

Jacob's burst into giggles was all Dan Fogler's idea. 'Everybody thought it was so funny [that] they kept it in,' says Katherine Waterston.

GOLDSTEIN SISTERS' HOT CHOCOLATE MUG CAKES

★

YIELD: 1 serving | PREP TIME: 5 minutes | COOK TIME: 1 minute

Newt Scamander and Jacob Kowalski find refuge at the Brooklyn apartment of Tina and Queenie Goldstein so they can regroup before looking for Newt's escaped beasts in *Fantastic Beasts and Where to Find Them*. The sisters' two small rooms are filled with personal items. 'I had imagined Queenie's life in my head,' says Alison Sudol, 'but to walk around in it was really something. You understand somebody on a very intimate level when you've been in their home.'

Katherine Waterston says seeing the row of books by Tina's bed was a grounding moment for her. 'It's so nice to have an environment that says so much about her. This was one of my favourite locations of the whole movie.'

This is an easy recipe if you have new friends, like Newt and Jacob, unexpectedly invited to your table: a chocolate mug cake made from scratch, featuring marshmallows and whipped cream. The flavour is rich with two kinds of chocolate, to approximate the flavour of cocoa. And unlike Newt and Jacob, who disappear into Newt's case that night, the marshmallows will remain visible after baking.

- 2 tablespoons plain flour
- 1 tablespoon soft light brown sugar
- 1 tablespoon cocoa powder
- ¼ teaspoon baking powder
- Pinch salt
- 2 tablespoons milk
- 1 tablespoon plus 1 teaspoon rapeseed oil
- ¼ teaspoon vanilla extract
- 1 tablespoon mini chocolate chips
- 1 heaped tablespoon mini marshmallows
- Whipped cream (optional)

In a microwave-safe mug, stir together the flour, brown sugar, cocoa powder, baking powder and salt. Make sure it's really well mixed. Add the milk, oil and vanilla extract. Stir well to combine, taking care to scrape the sides of the mug. Stir in the mini chocolate chips and mini marshmallows until just combined.

Microwave for 1 minute. Let sit for 2–3 minutes. Top with whipped cream, if desired, and enjoy immediately.

> **'BUT WE MADE 'EM COCOA.'**
>
> – Queenie Goldstein, *Fantastic Beasts and Where to Find Them*

Chapter Five

PARIS

BELOWGROUND BRIE EN CROÛTE

YIELD: 6 servings | PREP TIME: 15 minutes | COOK TIME: 25 minutes

---

Like the British Ministry of Magic, the French Ministry is belowground. In *Fantastic Beasts: The Crimes of Grindelwald*, Queenie Goldstein visits by entering a small square of trees. Magically, the roots of the trees rise up and form an Art Nouveau–style bird-cage lift that descends to the Ministry.

Art Nouveau was the prevalent design of Paris in the 1920s. '[But] Art Nouveau is all about light and nature and glass,' says assistant production designer Martin Foley, 'and the Ministry is underground. So we just ignored that fact.' The French Ministry was designed as a series of domed rooms set among connecting tunnels. 'Each of these domes has a glass ceiling, and they have an ethereal, magical glow,' he explains, 'so straight away, we almost forget we're underground.'

Just as the French Ministry of Magic is hidden from view, so is the incredible flavour that lies beneath the surface of this Brie en Croûte, which sits upon jam and bacon and is wrapped in puff pastry before being baked to gooey perfection.

4 rashers bacon

Flour, for dusting

1 sheet puff pastry, thawed

75g fig jam

1 Brie cheese wheel

FOR SERVING

Apple slices

Savoury biscuits

Baguette, sliced

Preheat the oven to 190°C/170°C fan/Gas Mark 5. Line a baking sheet with baking paper.

In a large frying pan over a medium heat, cook the bacon until browned, 5–6 minutes. Transfer the bacon to a kitchen paper–lined plate and leave to cool slightly before transferring it to a chopping board and chopping it into small pieces.

Dust a chopping board with flour. Lay the puff pastry on the prepared chopping board. Heap up the bacon in the centre. Place the fig jam on top. Top with the Brie wheel. Wrap the puff pastry up and around the Brie, moistening the edges with a little bit of water, as needed, to seal.

Bake for 20–25 minutes or until the puff pastry is browned and puffed. Serve with a cheese knife, for cutting and spreading, along with apple slices, savoury biscuits and a baguette, or whatever you like with Brie.

★ BEHIND THE MAGIC ★

Decorating the huge dome over the Ministry's main entrance is a celestial map. Unlike Muggle astronomical charts, this one features Hippogriffs and Kappas. Instead of a Capricorn, there is a Graphorn.

'*BIENVENUE AU MINISTÈRE DES AFFAIRES MAGIQUES.*'

– Receptionist, French Ministry of Magic, *Fantastic Beasts: The Crimes of Grindelwald*

NICOLAS FLAMEL'S CARAMELIZED ONION GALETTE

V | YIELD: 6 servings | PREP TIME: 15 minutes | COOK TIME: 1 hour 20 minutes

In *Fantastic Beasts: The Crimes of Grindelwald*, Newt, Tina, Jacob and Yusuf Kama visit Nicolas Flamel's house on Rue de Montmorency to regroup after a series of intense adventures. Flamel is the only known maker of the Philosopher's Stone, which creates the Elixir of Life and grants the creator immortality. At the time of their visit, Flamel is six hundred years old.

Filmmakers reasoned that Flamel's house was at least as old as him and thus designed it in the Tudor style. 'His house in Paris has been left behind,' says assistant production designer Martin Foley. 'But he knows where he is in time.' Actor Brontis Jodorowsky imagines that although Flamel still does research into alchemy, he uses only a small part of the house, which is apparent by the dust everywhere else.

This galette – a flat pastry that's usually round – is a flaky, free-form French dish with flair. Just as the act of alchemy turns an object into gold, caramelizing the onions turns them what cooks call 'gilded.' Add to that the garlic, spring onions and Gouda cheese, and this side dish will transform your dinner into something magical.

½ recipe for pastry from Hermione Granger's Extension Charm Bacon and Potato Pasties (see page 22)

Flour, for work surface

1 tablespoon olive oil

3 large sweet onions, thinly sliced (root to stalks)

1 teaspoon coarse salt

½ teaspoon sugar

1 tablespoon red wine

115g vintage Gouda cheese, grated

Line a baking sheet with baking paper.

Prepare the pastry and roll out on to a lightly floured surface. Place the pastry on baking paper and chill while preparing the filling.

Heat the olive oil in a large frying pan over a medium heat. Add the onions and spread into a thin layer. Cook 10 minutes without stirring. Season with the salt and sugar, stir and spread into a thin layer. Reduce the heat to medium-low. Cook, stirring only a few times, for 30 minutes. Add the red wine and stir to combine. Cook until the wine is absorbed, 3–5 minutes. Preheat the oven to 190°C/170°C fan/Gas Mark 5.

Remove the pastry from the refrigerator and top with the Gouda cheese (leaving a 2.5cm rim around the edges) and onions. Fold the rim over on to the filling.

Place the pie in the oven, and bake for 25–30 minutes or until golden. Cool for 10 minutes before slicing and serving.

> 'WHAT'S THAT?'
> 'IT'S AN ADDRESS OF A VERY OLD ACQUAINTANCE OF MINE. A SAFE HOUSE IN PARIS. REINFORCED WITH ENCHANTMENTS.'
>
> – Newt Scamander and Albus Dumbledore,
> *Fantastic Beasts: The Crimes of Grindelwald*

CAFÉ ABRINGER LA TARTINE PLATE

✴

V | YIELD: 6 servings | PREP TIME: 3 hours | COOK TIME: 1 hour

Tina Goldstein is reinstated as an Auror before the events of *Fantastic Beasts: The Crimes of Grindelwald*. She has gone to Paris to track down and help the Obscurial Credence, who has found shelter at the Circus Arcanus. Just as Tina locates him there she notices Yusuf Kama, who also seeks Credence. At a café in the Place Cachée, Kama shows her something that might aid Credence, as he is sought by several wizarding ministries.

Katherine Waterston (Tina) believes that her character is concerned about Credence and feels a responsibility to protect and take care of him, as she does her sister, Queenie. 'She'll break the rules to help protect any child,' says Waterston. 'I think that's what initially drew her to Credence.'

This crispy homemade baguette served with strawberry jam and butter is a simple but delicious dish that would be served at a Parisian café in either the wizarding world or the Non-Magique world at any time of day.

BREAD

350ml warm water

1 tablespoon sugar

1½ teaspoons coarse salt

2¼ teaspoons fast-action dried yeast

435g plain flour, plus more for dusting

Butter or oil, for greasing

TO MAKE THE BREAD:

In a large mixing bowl, stir together the water, sugar and salt. Scatter with the yeast and leave to sit for a few minutes until it has all foamed. Stir together. Add the flour all at once and stir to combine. The dough will be sticky and you may need to use wet hands to incorporate the last of the flour into it.

Transfer the dough to a large greased bowl and cover with a tea towel. Set in a warm, draught-free spot and leave to rise for at least 1 hour. The dough should double in size.

Line a baking sheet with baking paper and then use oil to grease the baking paper. Flour a chopping board; set aside.

Divide the dough in half. Transfer half of the dough to a floured board and use a rolling pin to roll it into a rectangle. (Tip: flour the dough and the rolling pin, and keep a dough scraper handy. This dough will still be really sticky.)

After it's rolled out, roll the dough into a log along the long side. Taper the ends by pinching them until they come to a point.

Place the loaf on the prepared baking sheet. Repeat with the second half of the dough. Cover both loaves with a clean tea towel and set in a warm, draught-free place to rise for at least 1 hour or until doubled in size.

Preheat the oven to 200°C/180°C fan/Gas Mark 6.

Using a serrated knife, cut three diagonal slits in the top of each loaf. Bake for 20–25 minutes until golden. Leave to cool.

Continued on page 197

Continued from page 194

JAM

300g strawberries, halved

100g granulated sugar

1 teaspoon lemon zest

Salted butter, for serving

TO MAKE THE JAM:

Combine the strawberries, sugar and lemon zest in a medium saucepan, stirring well to combine. Bring the mixture to the boil over a medium-high heat, stirring frequently. The fruit will release their juices as it cooks.

Reduce the heat to medium-low and simmer 40–45 minutes, stirring occasionally. The jam is done when it has thickened and a spoon leaves a wide wake when pushed through it.

Transfer to an airtight container and chill completely in the refrigerator, about 1 hour.

Slice the loaves and serve the sliced bread with the cooled jam and salted butter.

> **'I THINK WE WERE BOTH AT THE CIRCUS FOR THE SAME REASON. MONSIEUR...?'**
>
> – Tina Goldstein, *Fantastic Beasts: The Crimes of Grindelwald*

NON-MAGIQUE FRENCH BAKED CASSEROLE

✴

YIELD: 4 servings | PREP TIME: 15 minutes | COOK TIME: 1 hour

When Albus Dumbledore and Gellert Grindelwald were young, they wanted to change the wizarding world. But their ideas on the relationships between wizards and non-magical people – Muggles in the UK, No-Majs in North America and Non-Magiques in Paris – differed drastically, and the friends parted ways.

In *Fantastic Beasts: The Crimes of Grindelwald*, Grindelwald escapes his capture by MACUSA – the Magical Congress of the United States – in New York and travels to Paris, looking for the Obscurial Credence Barebone and gathering followers, including Queenie Goldstein. 'Grindelwald has his agenda,' says producer David Heyman. 'He is trying to build support and engineer events to help his cause for what he views as the "greater good", which is that the wizarding world will no longer have to be in secret, that it can emerge and be the dominating force in the world.'

In this flavourful French classic, chicken and sausage are browned and then cooked in a stock of tomatoes, vermouth and onions. Perhaps if Grindelwald had tried this, he would have understood that Non-Magiques have their own form of magic in flavourful, hearty dishes.

115g bacon, chopped

675g boneless, skinless chicken thighs

Salt

Pepper

2 tablespoons olive oil

1 brown onion, finely diced

2 carrots, peeled and diced

3 cloves garlic, very finely chopped

1 Polish kielbasa sausage, cut into 5mm slices

1 teaspoon dried thyme

1 bay leaf

250ml white wine

1 x 400g can cannellini beans

2 tablespoons tomato purée

250ml chicken stock

65g Italian breadcrumbs

FOR SERVING
Bread of your choice

Preheat the oven to 190°C/170°C fan/Gas Mark 5.

In a large oven-safe frying pan over a medium heat, cook the bacon until it is browned, 5–7 minutes. Transfer to a kitchen paper–lined plate, leaving the bacon fat in the pan.

Season the chicken thighs all over with salt and pepper. Add to the frying pan and increase the heat to medium-high. Do not crowd the chicken; it may need to be cooked in batches. Cook for 6 minutes, and then flip and cook for 4–5 minutes until cooked through. Transfer to a chopping board.

Add the olive oil, onion and carrots to the frying pan and fry, stirring occasionally, for 6–8 minutes until softened and the onion begins to turn golden. Add the garlic and sausage and warm for 2–3 minutes. Add the thyme, bay leaf, wine, beans, tomato purée and chicken stock. Stir well to combine. Reduce heat to just above low and simmer for 5 minutes.

Meanwhile, cut the chicken into bite-sized pieces. Stir into the frying pan. Top with the breadcrumbs and bacon. Place the frying pan in the oven and bake for 15 minutes or until bubbly. Serve with bread for sopping up the juices.

'THE MOMENT HAS COME TO SHARE MY VISION OF THE FUTURE THAT AWAITS IF WE DO NOT RISE UP AND TAKE OUR RIGHTFUL PLACE IN THE WORLD.'

– Gellert Grindelwald, *Fantastic Beasts: The Crimes of Grindelwald*

ZOUWU CHEESE SOUFFLÉ

YIELD: 4 servings | PREP TIME: 20 minutes | COOK TIME: 30 minutes

The Zouwu, a cat-like beast from Chinese mythology, is the size of an elephant, but it runs through the streets of Paris with a graceful airiness in *Fantastic Beasts: The Crimes of Grindelwald*. The Zouwu was captured and displayed at the Circus Arcanus before its escape. Because it was abused at the circus, the Zouwu is untrusting and angry until Newt comes to its aid.

For the film, the Zouwu went through several iterations as conceived by the development artists. Originally, it had tentacles around its neck, but those changed to become a mane like a lion's. Its plumed tail, which triples its length, floats behind it with the elegance and power of a kite's tail, keeping it buoyant as it leaps over bridges and bounces off buildings.

This airy egg dish is inspired by the fluffiness of the Zouwu. In this recipe, Gruyère cheese is seasoned with thyme and a touch of paprika. Light and flavourful, this soufflé might make you purr in delight.

40g unsalted butter, plus extra for greasing the pan

25g Parmesan cheese, grated

250ml milk

25g plain flour

½ teaspoon coarse salt, plus more to taste

¼ teaspoon pepper

1 teaspoon dried thyme

½ teaspoon paprika

9 medium egg yolks, at room temperature

115g Gruyère cheese, grated

5 medium egg whites, at room temperature

⅛ teaspoon cream of tartar

Preheat the oven to 200°C/180°C fan/Gas Mark 6.

Grease the inside of a 2-litre round baking dish (19cm in diameter and 8cm deep) with butter, and then scatter evenly with 1 tablespoon Parmesan cheese.

In a small saucepan over a medium heat, scald the milk –it should have tiny bubbles on the surface and be just short of boiling. Remove from the heat and set aside.

Melt the butter in a small saucepan over a low heat. Whisk in the flour and cook, whisking constantly, for 2 minutes. Remove from heat and whisk in the hot milk, salt, pepper, thyme and paprika. Return to the hob over a low heat and cook, whisking constantly, for 1 minute. The mixture should be smooth and thick.

Remove from heat and whisk in the egg yolks, one at a time. Add the Gruyère cheese and remaining Parmesan cheese and stir well. Transfer the mixture to a large mixing bowl.

In the bowl of a stand mixer or a large bowl if using a hand mixer, whisk the egg whites, the cream of tartar and a pinch of salt for 1 minute on low speed. Increase the speed to medium and beat for 1 minute. Then beat on high speed until firm, glossy peaks form, 3–4 minutes.

Puppeteers provided a soft foam mould of the Zouwu's head for Eddie Redmayne (Newt) to interact with after they bonded. 'They have this real big human and giant magical character cuddle,' says supervising creature puppeteer Robin Guiver.

Add one-quarterof the egg white mixture to the cheese mixture and whisk to combine. Add the remaining egg whites and fold in. Transfer to the prepared baking dish and smooth the top. Draw a large circle around the outer edge of the mixture with a spatula to help the soufflé rise.

Place in the centre of the oven. Reduce the heat to 190°C/170°C fan/ Gas Mark 5. Bake for 25–30 minutes or until puffed and brown.

Serve immediately.

> **'WELL, THAT'LL BE THE ZOUWU.'**
>
> – Newt Scamander, *Fantastic Beasts: The Crimes of Grindelwald*

JACOB KOWALSKI'S PLEA FOR PAIN AU CHOCOLAT

✳

V | YIELD: 8 servings | PREP TIME: 45 minutes | COOK TIME: 15–20 minutes

Newt Scamander and Jacob Kowalski take a Portkey to Paris in *Fantastic Beasts: The Crimes of Grindelwald* and travel to Place Cachée, the Parisian equivalent of Diagon Alley. There, Newt uses Appare Vestigium, a locating spell, to find Credence. When Newt races away in pursuit of a clue, Jacob chases after him, not unaware of the cafés and their tempting fare lining the street, in the hope that Newt will honour his request to take a break and enjoy one of Paris's most popular pastries.

Like Diagon Alley, Place Cachée has a Quidditch shop, a wand shop and an apothecary. There is also a sweet shop, Enchanted Confectionery. 'I just felt, there was one in Diagon Alley, and it would be rude not to!' says set decorator Anna Pinnock.

The warm, buttery taste of a crusty croissant-type wrapper around a thick ribbon of sweet chocolate makes Pain au Chocolat ('bread with chocolate') a treat worth stopping for.

115g dark chocolate (70% cocoa), roughly chopped

60ml whipping cream

1 egg and 1 tablespoon water, for egg wash

400g puff pastry, thawed

30g icing sugar

✳ **BEHIND THE MAGIC** ✳

Chaudrons, the French twin to Diagon Alley's cauldron shop, sells copper moulds for food.

Line a baking sheet with baking paper or a silicone baking mat. In a microwave-safe bowl, add the chocolate and cover it with the cream. Microwave for 1 minute; then leave to stand for 5 minutes. Stir until completely smooth and then pour out on to the prepared baking sheet. Using a spatula, gently shape the chocolate into a roughly 15 x 10cm rectangle. Chill in the refrigerator for 30 minutes.

Preheat the oven to 220°C/200°C fan/Gas Mark 7. Whisk the egg and water to create the egg wash. Set aside.

On a lightly floured surface, roll out the puff pastry to a 33 x 28cm rectangle and cut it into eighths (about 12.5 x 7.5cm pieces). Sift a light dusting of the icing sugar over the top. Remove the chocolate mixture from the refrigerator and cut it into eighths. Cover the baking sheet in a clean piece of baking paper or a baking mat.

Place 1 piece of chocolate in the centre of each puff pastry piece. Take one end, about a third, and fold it over the chocolate. Brush this with some egg wash and sift another light dusting of icing sugar over the top. Fold the other end over this, like folding a letter; brush with more egg wash and sift more icing sugar over the top. Using a spatula, transfer to the baking sheet. Repeat with all the pieces. Bake for 20–25 minutes or until the pastry is puffed and golden. Leave to cool for at least 5 minutes until serving. Leftovers can be stored in an airtight container for up to 3 days.

FLAMING PHOENIX COCKTAILS

V, V+, GF | YIELD: 4 servings | PREP TIME: 10 minutes

The phoenix bird is continually reborn. At the end of each life cycle, it erupts into flames and then rises up from the ashes of that fire. Albus Dumbledore has a phoenix named Fawkes, first seen in *Harry Potter and the Chamber of Secrets*. It was a given that Fawkes would be the colour of fire, with his top mainly burnt oranges and dark reds. At his last stage of life, he has the colouring of a burned-out match, with the last embers of brilliance around his eyes.

Phoenixes are tied to the Dumbledore family; once Credence joins Gellert Grindelwald in *Fantastic Beasts: The Crimes of Grindelwald*, the Dark wizard shows the young man a phoenix chick. He tosses it into the air, where it grows to full size and lights on fire, reborn. This confirms to Credence that he is actually a Dumbledore. This fiery drink will bring every party or occasion to life over and over again.

1 lime

2 tablespoons red sparkle sugar (optional)

125ml triple sec

60ml grenadine

60ml lime juice

60ml vanilla syrup

125ml spiced rum

SPECIALIST TOOLS
Coupe glasses

Cut ½ lime into 4 thin slices, for garnish, and set aside. Cut the remaining half of the lime into wedges and run them around the rim of each glass. Pour the sugar on to a shallow plate and twist the rim of each glass in the sugar until it is well coated.

In a medium jug, add the triple sec, grenadine, lime juice, vanilla syrup and rum. Stir and divide the liquid among the glasses. Top each with a lime slice.

> 'THERE IS A LEGEND IN YOUR FAMILY THAT A PHOENIX WILL COME TO ANY MEMBER WHO IS IN DIRE NEED.'
>
> – Gellert Grindelwald to Credence, *Fantastic Beasts: The Crimes of Grindelwald*

★ BEHIND THE MAGIC ★

As Credence and Dumbledore duel in *Fantastic Beasts: The Secrets of Dumbledore*, a grey-coloured phoenix circles overhead. 'It does look a little bit worse for wear,' says visual effects supervisor Christian Manz. 'As it flies, flames come from its wings, and it drops ash everywhere.'

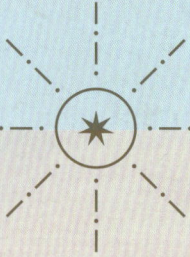

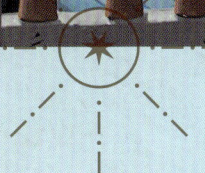

SUGGESTED MENUS

Harry Potter Film Night

Vanishing Crispy Cauliflower and Leek Fritters (page 74)

Niffler Babies' Everything Chicken Wings (page 162)

Luchino Caffe Picante Paninis (page 37)

Halloween Pumpkin Carrot Squares (page 101)

Mooncalf Moon Cake Sandwiches (page 174)

Yule Ball Sherbet Fizzy (page 87)

Harry Potter Cocktail Party

Professor Slughorn's Dinner Party Sausage Rolls (page 62)

Slug Club Prawn and Chorizo Skewers (page 65)

Belowground Brie en Croûte (page 190)

Hogsmeade Ginger and Lime Butterscotch Mug (page 96)

Professor Lupin's Full Moon Spritzer (page 88)

The Blind Pig Laughing Lemonade Cocktails (page 181)

Bill and Fleur's Wedding Chocolate Puffs (page 52)

Get Well Half Moon Biscuits (page 121)

Harry Potter Halloween Party

Dudley Dursley's Swirly Tail Bacon Cheddar Breadsticks (page 14)

Hermione Granger's Extension Charm Bacon and Potato Pasties (page 22)

Harry Potter's Late Night Split Pea Soup (page 21)

All Better Now Chocolate Cakes (page 38)

Weasley and Weasley Inspired Fudge (page 114)

Hagrid's Perfect Pumpkin Smoothies (page 92)

Hogwarts Hot Mulled Pumpkin Cider (page 100)

Holiday Party

MACUSA Codfish Cakes (page 163)

Sorting Hat Ceremony Peas, Bacon and Diced Onions (page 144)

Argus Filch and Mrs Norris's Roasted Garlic Mashed Butternut Squash (page 153)

Arthur Weasley's Muggle-Inspired Baked Gnocchi Casserole (page 44)

End-of-Year Feast Beef Short Ribs with Yorkshire Pudding and Buttery Diced Carrots (page 138)

Ginny Weasley's Star Sugar Tartlets (page 48)

Triwizard Champions Cake (page 103)

Flaming Phoenix Cocktails (page 204)

· ·

Picnic in the Park

Jacob's Kowalski's Plea for Pain au Chocolat (page 203)

Nimbus 2000 Toasted Parmesan Brooms with Pine Nut Roasted Garlic Hummus (page 66)

Nicholas Flamel's Caramelized Onion Galette (page 193)

Wizard Chess Chessboard Biscuits (page 117)

Hogsmeade Ginger and Lime Butterscotch Mug (page 96)

RECIPES ORGANIZED BY TYPE

Mains

Desserts

Drinks

DIETARY CONSIDERATIONS

V: Vegetarian
V*: Easily made vegetarian
V+: Vegan
V+*: Easily made vegan
GF: Gluten-free
GF*: Easily made gluten-free

Chapter One
LONDON, LITTLE WHINGING & THE BURROW

Dudley Dursley's Swirly Tail Bacon Cheddar Breadsticks

Xenophilius Lovegood's Tea Bread: V

On the Run Flapjacks: V, GF

Hermione Granger's Extension Charm Bacon and Potato Pasties

Order of the Phoenix Citrus Bread: V

The Burrow Currant Scones: V

Dudley's Special Day Breakfast: GF*

Leaky Cauldron Tomato Chicken Stew

Harry Potter's Late Night Split Pea Soup: V, V+*, GF

Diagon Alley Steak and Ale Pie

Surbiton Smoked Ham Toasties: GF*

Luchino Caffe Picante Paninis: GF*

Owl Post Chicken Parcels

Arthur Weasley's Baked Muggle Gnocchi Casserole

The Burrow Meat Slices

Shell Cottage Seed Bread: V

Hogsmeade Ginger and Lime Butterscotch Mug: V, V+, GF

Ginny Weasley's Star Sugar Tartlets: V

Bill and Fleur's Wedding Chocolate Puffs: V

All Better Now Chocolate Cakes: V

Chapter Two
HOGWARTS

Professor Slughorn's Dinner Party Sausage Rolls

Nimbus 2000 Toasted Parmesan Brooms with Pine Nut Roasted Garlic Hummus

Vanishing Crispy Cauliflower and Leek Fritters: V

Slug Club Prawn and Chorizo Skewers

Goblet of Fire Scotch Pancakes with Warm, Buttery Maple Syrup: V

Quidditch Eggs on Toast for the Win: GF*

Great Hall Sweet French Toast with Berry Compote: V

Ron Weasley's Breakup Chicken Noodle Soup

Room of Requirement Meatballs in Red Wine Sauce

Professor Sprout's Vegetable Patch Tart: V

Unicorns of the Forbidden Forest Changing Vermicelli Noodle Chicken Salad: GF*

Yule Ball Sherbet Fizzy: V, GF

Professor Lupin's Full Moon Spritzer: V, V+, GF

WonderWitch Passion Juice Smoothie: V, V+, GF

Hagrid's Perfect Pumpkin Smoothies: V, GF

Sorting Hat Sips: V, GF*

Ron's Lucky Day Slurp: V, V+, GF

Hogwarts Hot Mulled Pumpkin Cider: V, V+, GF

Chapter Three
GREAT HALL FEASTS

Chapter Four
NEW YORK CITY

Chapter Five
PARIS

MEASUREMENT CONVERSION

Kitchen Measurements

MILLILITRES	UK FL OZ	SPOONS	US CUPS
15ml	½fl oz	3 tsp/1 tbsp	1/16 cup
30ml	1fl oz	2 tbsp	⅛ cup
60ml	2fl oz	4 tbsp	¼ cup
80ml	2¾fl oz	5½ tbsp	⅓ cup
120ml	4fl oz	8 tbsp	½ cup
160ml	5½fl oz	10⅔ tbsp	⅔ cup
180ml	6½fl oz	12 tbsp	¾ cup
240ml	8½fl oz	16 tbsp	1 cup

ML/LITRES	UK FL OZ	UK PINTS	US CUPS	US FL OZ
300ml	10½fl oz	½ pint	1¼ cups	10fl oz
568ml	20fl	1 pint	2⅜ cups	19¼fl oz
1 litre	35fl oz	1¾ pints	4¼ cups	34fl oz
1.2 litres	42¼fl oz	2 pints	5 cups	40½fl oz
2 litres	70fl oz	3½ pints	8½ cups	67½fl oz

Weight

GRAMS	OUNCES
15g	½oz
28–30g	1oz
55g	2oz
85g	3oz
115g	4oz
140g	5oz
175g	6oz
285g	10oz
400g	14oz
450g	16oz
900g	32oz

Oven Temperatures

CELSIUS	FAHRENHEIT
95°C	200°F
110°C	225°F
120°C	250°F
140°C	275°F
150°C	300°F
160°C	325°F
180°C	350°F
190°C	375°F
200°C	400°F
220°C	425°F
230°C	450°F

Length

METRIC	IMPERIAL
2.5cm	1in
5cm	2in
10cm	4in
15cm	6in
20cm	8in
25cm	10in
30cm	12in

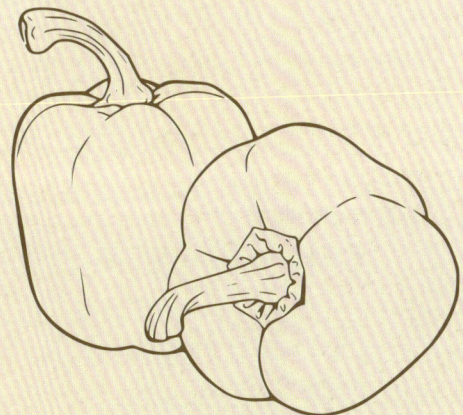

GLOSSARY

Baking paper: Food-safe paper that can withstand temperatures of up to 230°C/210°C fan/Gas Mark 8 – even higher for short baking times – that's used to line pans for baking and roasting. Baking paper prevents foods sticking and makes washing up easier.

Beat: To blend ingredients and/or incorporate air into a mixture by vigorously whisking, stirring or using a handheld or stand mixer.

Blender: Blends or purées sauces and soups to varying textures, from chunky to perfectly smooth. Also use to make smoothies and shakes.

Butter: Unless otherwise noted, recipes call for salted butter.

Butterfly Pea Flowers: These dried flower blossoms are commonly used in herbal tea drinks. When added to a recipe, they provide a beautiful deep blue colour. If combined with acids such as lemon juice, the colour turns to pink or purple. They are available online and in some health-food shops. They are also turned into a powder and an extract.

Casserole: A large (usually 5- to 6-litre) oven-proof glass dish or heavy metal cooking pot ideal for making stews, braises and deep-fried foods on the hob or in the oven. Casseroles made from cast iron or enamelled cast iron will hold and distribute heat evenly. A casserole works well when cooking with both high and low temperatures, making it a versatile vessel and handy addition to every kitchen.

Caster Sugar: The same thing as granulated sugar but caster sugar has smaller granules, making it a better choice for baking. To make your own, blitz an equivalent quantity of granulated sugar in a stand mixer or food processor for 1 minute.

Colander: Separates liquids from solids by draining the liquid through the small holes in the bowl.

Cutting in Butter: To work cold butter into dry ingredients to break it down into small pea-sized pieces and disperse it evenly throughout the mixture. The butter must be very cold so it does not begin to soften. These little pieces of butter surrounded by the dry ingredients are what create the flakiness in pastry.

Egg Wash: A mixture used to create a sheen or gloss on breads, pastries and other baked goods. Whisk together 1 egg and 1 tablespoon of water until light and foamy. Use a pastry brush to apply before baking when the recipe requires.

Folding In: Gently adding an ingredient with a spatula in wide gentle strokes. Do not whisk or stir vigorously. Folding allows any airiness already established to stay intact.

Food Processor: A motorized machine with a bowl and a series of removable blades used for chopping, shredding, slicing and blending ingredients. A food processor can be used to prepare vegetables, fruits and cheeses for cooking as well as blending sauces and dips.

Frying Pan: Shallow round cooking vessel used primarily for stovetop cooking. It's good to have a range of sizes. Generally, a small frying pan is 15cm across, a medium frying pan is 20cm across, a large frying pan is 25cm across and an extra large frying pan is 30cm across.

Granulated Sugar: A highly refined sugar made from sugar cane or beetroot known for its white colour and fine texture. The molasses has been removed from this type of sugar.

Greasing a Tin: Coating a tin with non-stick cooking spray, oil, softened butter or fat to stop (usually) bakes such as cakes sticking.

Hand-held Mixer: A lightweight hand-held machine with removable attachments used for blending and whipping eggs, cake batters and lighter weight, less-dense doughs.

High-Heat vs Non-stick Cookware: A high-heat pot or pan – as its name suggests – can stand up to high-heat cooking, generally temperatures of 200°C/180°C fan/Gas Mark 6 and above. They are usually made of stainless steel, cast iron or enamelled cast iron and can be used on the hob or oven – if the handle is made of an ovenproof material. Non-stick cookware contains a coating that helps keeps foods sticking (particularly eggs), but they cannot be used at the same temperatures as high-heat pans. If you are cooking with non-stick cookware, make sure you know the manufacturer's heat limits for your cookware. Most non-stick cookware should not be used at above medium heat on a hob (about 180°C) and is not generally suitable for the oven.

Icing sugar: This is granulated sugar that has been ground into a powdered state. It's primarily used to make smooth icings and for dusting finished baked goods.

Kitchen Scales: Used for measuring ingredients by weight. Look for an electronic digital scale calibrated to 0.1g up to 5kg for precise quantities, which is essential for baking.

Measuring Jug: Clear glass or plastic jug for measuring precise amounts of liquids by lining up the level of liquid to the marks on the cup. Useful sizes include 250ml, 500ml and 1 litre.

Measuring Spoons: A set of measuring tools used to accurately portion smaller amounts of ingredients. They usually come in a set that includes ⅛ teaspoon, ¼ teaspoon, ½ teaspoon, 1 teaspoon and 1 tablespoon. They can be used for liquid ingredients such as vinegar, juices, oils and extracts and dry ingredients such as flour, salt, sugar and spices.

Milk: Unless otherwise noted, these recipes call for dairy milk. In most cases, any percentage of milk fat will do, unless otherwise noted.

Muddle: A long-handled tool with a textured end, used to mash together ingredients such as fruits, herbs and sugar when making drinks.

Peeling Ginger: To peel fresh ginger root, use the edge of a small spoon to scrape away the peel. This keeps the root intact, with less waste, and allows you to easily navigate the lumps and bumps.

Piping Icing: The process of decorating cakes and biscuits by squeezing icing from a piping bag. Piping can be done with or without a nozzle – or even in a plastic bag with one corner snipped off to allow the icing to be applied in a neat rope shape.

Rolling Pin: A long, cylindrical tool – most often made of wood – used to flatten and roll out dough when making breads and pastries.

Rubber Spatula: A handled tool with a flat, flexible blade used to fold ingredients together and to scrape the sides of bowls clean.

Salt: Unless otherwise noted, use your salt of choice in the recipes in this book. Coarse salt – which is coarser than regular table salt – is the type of salt that is most commonly used throughout the book.

Saucepan with Lid: Round deep cooking vessel used for boiling or simmering. It is useful to have a range of sizes, from small 0.9 litre (14cm) pans to large 3.8 litre (20cm) pans.

Sear: To create a crust on a piece of meat, poultry or fish by placing it in a very hot pan or on a very hot grill. The high heat quickly caramelizes the natural sugars in the food, creating a deeply browned and flavourful crust. Once the crust is formed, the heat is usually turned down so that the interior of the meat can cook properly before the outside is burned.

Sift: The process of putting flour, icing sugar or cornflour through a fine-mesh sieve to aerate and remove lumps. Multiple ingredients – such as flour, salt and leavenings – are often sifted together to blend them.

Silicone Baking Mat: Used to line shallow baking tins when making foods such as biscuits and pastries to prevent sticking. They can withstand high temperatures in the oven and can also be used in the freezer. Dough can be rolled out on them, and they can easily go from prep station to chilling to the oven without having to move the dough. They are easy to clean and reusable.

Simmer: To cook a liquid such as a sauce or soup at low-enough heat so that bubbles are just barely breaking over the surface.

Spatula/Fish Slice: A handled tool with a wide, flexible blade used to flip or turn foods during cooking.

Stand Mixer: A heavy-duty machine with a large bowl and various attachments used to mix, beat or whip foods at varying speeds. Stand mixers are necessary for making heavy, dense or stiff doughs for biscuits or yeasted breads.

Stick blender: A slender style of hand-held mixer used for puréeing soups and sauces in the pot.

Sugar Thermometer: Sometimes called a candy thermometer, a long glass thermometer that can be clipped to the side of a pot. It can withstand temperatures of at least 260°C and is used to measure the temperatures of frying oil or sugar when making syrups, boiled sweets and certain icings.

Vanilla Bean Paste vs Vanilla Extract: Vanilla bean paste provides strong vanilla flavour and beautiful vanilla bean flecks without having to split and scrape a vanilla pod (aka vanilla bean). While it is more expensive than extract, there are situations in which it really elevates the finished dish. When that is the case, a recipe will specifically call for vanilla bean paste, but it can always be replaced in a 1-to-1 ratio with vanilla extract.

Whip: To use a whisk or electric mixer to aerate ingredients such as egg whites and double cream to lighten, stiffen and form peaks.

Whisk: A handled tool with thin wires arranged in various shapes used for mixing and whipping liquids and batters to combine ingredients or incorporate air into them. The two most common types of whisks are the balloon whisk, which has a bulbous end that narrows down towards the handle and the sauce whisk, which has a round coil that sits flat on the bottom of the pan.

INDEX

220

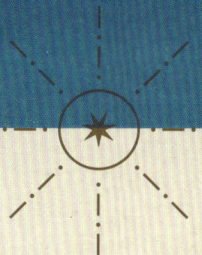

![greenfinch logo]

greenfinch

First published in Great Britain in 2024 by
Greenfinch
An imprint of Quercus Editions Ltd
Carmelite House
50 Victoria Embankment
London EC4Y 0DZ
An Hachette UK company

All rights reserved. Published by arrangement with Insight Editions,
LP, 800 A Street, San Rafael, CA 94901, USA
www.insighteditions.com

ISBN: 978-1-52943-503-0

Publisher: Raoul Goff
VP, Group Publisher: Vanessa Lopez
VP, Creative: Chrissy Kwasnik
VP, Manufacturing: Alix Nicholaeff
Senior Designer: Lola Villanueva
Senior Editor: Anna Wostenberg
Editorial Assistants: Sami Alvarado, Alecsander Zapata
VP, Senior Executive Project Editor: Vicki Jaeger
Production Associate: Deena Hashem
Senior Production Manager, Subsidiary Rights: Lina s Palma-Temena
Photoshoot and Illustration Art Direction: Judy Wiatrek Trum
Photographer: Ted Thomas
Food and Prop Stylist: Elena P. Craig
Assistant Food Stylist: Lauren Tedeschi
Assistant Food Stylist: Patricia Parrish
Cover and Interior Illustrations by Paula Hanback

ROOTS OF PEACE   🌐 REPLANTED PAPER

Insight Editions, in association with Roots of Peace, will plant two trees
for each tree used in the manufacturing of this book. Roots of Peace
is an internationally renowned humanitarian organization dedicated
to eradicating land mines worldwide and converting war-torn lands
into productive farms and wildlife habitats. Roots of Peace will plant
two million fruit and nut trees in Afghanistan and provide farmers
there with the skills and support necessary for sustainable land use.

Manufactured in China by Insight Editions

10 9 8 7 6 5 4 3 2 1

CONCEPT ART:

Page 2: Harry, Hermione and Ron approach the Lovegood House, carefully staying off the Dirigible Plums, in artwork by Adam Brockbank for *Harry Potter and the Deathly Hallows – Part 1*.

Pages 6–7: Andrew Williamson offers the alternate possibility of Molly Weasley watching Ron and Harry's approach to The Burrow in Arthur Weasley's Flying Ford Anglia car in *Harry Potter and the Chamber of Secrets*. In the film, they are already inside the house before she confronts them.

Page 9: Students are gathering into the Great Hall for protection against the fugitive Sirius Black in *Harry Potter and the Prisoner of Azkaban*. This is a composite of a film still and digital art of the ceiling's celestial sky by Dermot Power.

Pages 56–57: On a field trip to Hogsmeade, Harry, Ron and Hermione watch as Professor McGonagall and Hagrid enter The Three Broomsticks, painted for *Harry Potter and the Prisoner of Azkaban* by Andrew Williamson.

Page 96: The interior of The Hog's Head is given the view from the bartender's perspective in artwork by Andrew Williamsons for *Harry Potter and the Order of the Phoenix*.

Pages 124–125: Concept art of the towers of Hogwarts by Andrew Williamson for *Harry Potter and the Half-Blood Prince*.

Pages 154–155: Fred and George Weasley make an explosive exit from Hogwarts during O.W.L.'s exams in *Harry Potter and the Order of the Phoenix*. Artwork by Andrew Williamson.

Page 179: Artist Molly Sole found designing the droppings of the Mooncalves apparent in this piece for *Fantastic Beasts and Where to Find Them* to be an exciting and bizarre assignment.

Pages 184–185: Attention to detail and an accuracy of architecture were important to artist Peter Popken in the visual development art of a New York street for *Fantastic Beasts and Where to Find Them*.

Pages 206–207: Credence Barebone and the Maledictus-cursed Nagini seek refuge on a Paris rooftop in art by Peter Popken for *Fantastic Beasts: The Crimes of Grindelwald*.

Page 210: Harry and Hermione hike up the snow-filled streets of Hogsmeade towards The Three Broomsticks, where they will meet up with Professor Slughorn in *Harry Potter and the Half-Blood Prince*. Artwork by Andrew Williamson.

Page 222–223: Concept art of the Flying Ford Anglia carrying Ron and Harry arriving at Hogwarts by Dermot Power for *Harry Potter and the Chamber of Secrets*.

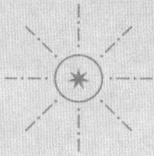

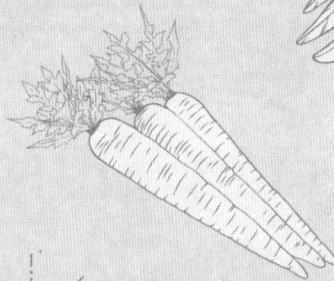